GOD KNOWS YOUR NAME

"God Knows Your Name *is an exceptional book. Through superb storytelling, Catherine Campbell makes the glorious truth of Isaiah 43:1 luminous for everyone: 'Fear not, for I have redeemed you; I have called you by your name.' Using both contemporary testimonies and Bible stories – artfully retold – Catherine Campbell brings us to a renewed sense of identity and significance under the Father's radiant smile.*

"This is a great book; you will laugh and weep in equal measure as you read it. I highly recommend it, especially for anyone who may be doubting their worth. This book is a powerful antidote to shame. I couldn't put it down."

Mark Stibbe, The Father's House Trust

"Catherine Campbell is a great storyteller. On a packed, noisy train, I found myself engrossed and deeply moved by a host of vivid, contemporary characters, past and present, who stayed with me long after my journey came to an end."

Michele Guinness

"A real page-turner: I really enjoyed this book and can certainly recommend it! Catherine brings Bible stories vividly to life, skilfully and powerfully combining them with parallel stories from the present day of those who have experienced the pain of rejection but have also found God's restoring embrace. This is a powerful book and deserves to be widely read!"

Wendy Virgo, Newfrontiers

"This book reveals God as 'I AM'. Through stories spanning 4,000 years, God moves from past doctrine to present reality."

Valerie Murphy, National Director of Precept, Northern Ireland

"This book is a joy to read. Catherine's refreshing insight into biblical situations, paralleled by gripping contemporary stories, turns our hearts to God in gratitude and awe."

Jean Gibson, author of *Seasons of Womanhood*

Other books by Catherine Campbell:

Under the Rainbow, Ambassador 2008

Rainbows for Rainy Days, Ambassador 2008

To find out more about the author go to

www.catherine-campbell.com

God knows *your* name

In a world of rejection, he accepts you

Catherine Campbell

MONARCH
BOOKS

Oxford, UK & Grand Rapids, Michigan, USA

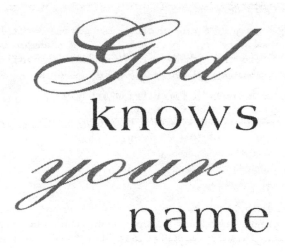

First published in the UK in 2010 by Monarch Books
(a publishing imprint of Lion Hudson plc)
Wilkinson House, Jordan Hill Road, Oxford OX2 8DR, England
Tel: +44 (0)1865 302750 Fax: +44 (0)1865 302757
Email: monarch@lionhudson.com
www.lionhudson.com

ISBN 978 1 85424 983 8

Distributed by:
UK: Marston Book Services, PO Box 269, Abingdon, Oxon, OX14 4YN
USA: Kregel Publications, PO Box 2607, Grand Rapids, Michigan 49501

The text paper used in this book has been made from wood independently certified as having come from sustainable forests.

British Library Cataloguing Data
A catalogue record for this book is available from the British Library.

Printed and bound in the UK by CPI Cox & Wyman, Reading.

Dedicated to Lorraine,
my sister, friend, and ever an advocate for the underdog!
Thank you for being such an inspiration.

Contents

Prologue

The evening had started badly. My transport hadn't turned up and I had no contact number to remedy the situation. Sitting on the edge of my bed in a posh B&B, I was all dressed up with nowhere to go. I had all but given up on what had promised to be a night to remember when a car suddenly screeched into the driveway, its tyres flinging gravel against the rose bushes. Apologizing profusely for "forgetting all about me", my hostess sped off in the direction of Wentworth Golf Club, muttering assurances about arriving in time for the banquet.

Her rather ordinary Vauxhall Astra looked totally out of place as she drove past an array of Jaguars, BMWs, and top-of-the-range sports cars to drop me off at the front door of the splendid cream-coloured building that was the Wentworth Clubhouse. Wentworth, hidden in the luxurious setting of Virginia Water in Surrey, England, is home to the rich and famous, whose mansions peek out from among the trees that line the winding road to the famous golf course. Competitions such as the Seniors Masters suit the setting just as perfectly as those held in Augusta; it is certainly a place of outstanding beauty.

On this particular occasion the golf competition was a celebrity charity event to raise funds for a proposed children's hospice in Northern Ireland. The event was called "Tee off for Joy", and Joy was our little girl; hence my presence.

With not a minute to spare I was whisked to my table, and placed beside the hospice project director and his wife, whom I knew well. Thankfully, my table etiquette was adequate, as I don't ever remember seeing such an array of place settings before or since. Everyone was seated apart from two places at our table, which I quickly learned was the top table. The seat beside me was empty, as was the one beside our host, Sir Alfred Dunhill, the clothing tycoon. The buzz in the room was electrifying, and glancing around it was clear to see that it was literally chock-a-block with sporting personalities, television celebrities, comedians and wealthy business people.

The latecomers arrived to a little friendly banter as they walked through the elegant dining room to take their places. The tall gentleman stretched out his hand as he sat beside me: "Bruce Forsyth," he said, "so nice to meet you. And you are…?"

"Catherine Campbell," I replied, trying not to look surprised to be talking to the most recognized face in British entertainment.

"I don't recognize your name. Should I know you?" he replied, looking puzzled.

"I doubt it. I'm here with the Children's Hospice delegation."

"Nice… and what do you do?"

"I work as a nurse in Northern Ireland."

"Nice... and what does your husband do?" he asked, fishing for any hint that I was someone of note.

"He's an evangelist; a Christian preacher."

"Oh," he mumbled.

My husband's job title killed the conversation in a flash, and I think he was more delighted to see the soup arriving than I was. Lady Dunhill, seated to his right, seemed quite happy to occupy "Brucie" for the rest of the evening with the kind of conversation that he was used to.

It was a surreal evening.

The food was superb; a visual as well as a culinary masterpiece, served by staff wearing white gloves; there were no smudges on these shiny plates. But it was the people-watching that made the evening for me, and the opportunity to hear what the rich and famous talk about. Personal trainers, hairdressers, the inability to get good staff these days, their pets, and the stupidity of one spotty teenager at a filling station not to recognize a £10,000 watch when it was left as guarantee for a £5 fill-up of petrol!

I felt alien in this world, where your name or position was of paramount importance and was reflected in the amount of attention you received. No sentence was wasted. Every word was used to bolster your importance with others: perhaps the next television appearance depended on it. Even the charity auction was a time for displaying financial muscle.

During the evening there were times when I felt insignificant. My little summer dress from Primark probably puzzled those trying to identify which designer was flavour of the month. Talk of interior designers, holiday homes on the

Costa somewhere and a myriad of other conversations that I couldn't enter into only reinforced the truth that I was a working class girl and they were out of my league.

The lifestyles of the rich and famous has become a national fascination. The media have opened up their world for us to look inside, consequently making us feel inferior and discontented. Sometimes we look at others and wish we could be like them. Even in our own circles there are people who just ooze popularity: anyone who is anyone knows them. Conversely, no one even seems to remember your name! If you fell off the planet, would anyone notice?

The desire to be recognized – or even merely to fit in – is endemic in our society today; though neither seems to bring lasting satisfaction. Yet as I left Wentworth that night, I was gripped by a far more amazing reality than spending the evening with people who would never need to wear a name badge. In the quietness of my B&B I reminded myself of God's words to Moses in Exodus 33:17b (NKJV): "For you have found grace in my sight, and I know you by name."

What an overwhelming thought. God knows my name!

In a world filled with rejection, sometimes purely on the basis that no one knows our names, we are known to the God who created us and who gave up his Son to die for us on Calvary. We do not need to struggle to gain recognition in heaven. Our names are already "written on his hands".

Nameless

c. 865 BC

"Why aren't you here when I need you so much? I can't do this alone. It's too hard."

Sadness mixed with disappointment, as the woman bent down to pick up a little wicker basket; her black skirts stirring up the dust from the dirt floor. In her mind's eye she could see her husband's handsome face set in a frame of black curls, dark dancing eyes smiling back at her. Then suddenly, just as she thought she could reach out and touch him, the comforting picture was gone again. Sometimes she was afraid that perhaps a day would come when she wouldn't remember him so easily. Yet how could that be, when she still loved him so much?

"How could you leave us? How could the gods punish us so by taking you from us?" she muttered to herself, as she turned towards a pile of old rags lying on top of a makeshift bed. From beneath them she heard a weak little voice cry: "Mama!" As she moved the rags aside, a smaller version of the picture from her memory looked up at her, his brown eyes sunken in his head and his dark curls lank and dull.

"It is OK, my son; I'm just going outside to gather some sticks. When I return I will make some bread for us. You rest for a little while longer."

"Will Papa come too?"

"No, my son, Papa cannot come to us now… the gods will not allow it. Rest now. Soon I will return."

Her thin fingers gently twisted his curls as he snuggled down among the rags once more. Soon her darling little boy was asleep and she felt it was safe to leave the house to look for sticks. She hated leaving him when he was so weak, but the fire pit was now cold and the last of her dung pats used up. Heading outside, she wrapped a tattered shawl around her shoulders, hoping to find a few sticks to fuel a fire that would allow her to feed her son for one last time.

Her heart felt too heavy to carry with her. The weight of it bowed her head lower than usual as she put her foot out into the narrow street. Neighbours didn't seem to suit the name any more. Since her husband died they had acted as if she didn't exist, passing her in the street without so much as a sympathetic look. Had everyone forgotten her name? No one seemed to use it any more. In some ways she understood: life was tough for everyone in Zarephath since the drought of neighbouring Israel had started to touch their borders, but as a widow there was no one left to help meet the needs of her family. All she had left was the hope that her little boy would die before she did. She dreaded the thought that he might be left to face death alone.

The breeze from the nearby harbour cooled her hot skin as she stepped over the open drains that wound their way through the narrow alleys of the walled city. The merchant ships still sailed into the distance, laden with trees, ceramics and the red-purple dye that brought Phoenicia its fame. But each time they returned they brought less and less food, as Israel was unable to meet the trade agreements set up years before, because of failing harvests. No rain meant no harvest. No husband meant no employment and nothing to barter with, which in turn meant no food.

As she passed the shrine to Astarte, wife of the Baal god Hadad, she grumbled, complaining about all that she had sacrificed there to this goddess of love and war. It appeared that Astarte favoured war over love, as she had ignored the pleas for healing for her husband.

"The grain sacrifices would have been better used to feed my son than to be wasted on a god who only brings heartache."

She now cared little if Astarte heard her. The Baals might promise to be the bringers of life, but she hadn't seen it in her home.

Reaching the city gate, the noise of the traders in the square served only to amplify the nothingness she felt inside. Guilt dogged her steps as she watched others buying and selling from the stalls, still able to provide for their families. Even the cows and camels had food of sorts. The laughter of everyday living mocked her. Joy was an emotion she hadn't felt for a long time, while sadness and despair were her daily companions. A few sticks lay unclaimed beside the gate and she bent towards the ground to pick them up.

"Please, bring me a little drink of water in a cup," said an unfamiliar voice behind her.

Turning to see who was speaking to her, she saw a foreigner coming through the city gate. To be truthful, he looked more like a vagrant than a respectable traveller. His clothes were dishevelled and his hair matted. His unkempt appearance told the story of a long journey, with as much dust on his body as on the road he had travelled. An Israelite, she reckoned; escaping from the famine, she thought. Yet inside lingered a strange feeling that she was somehow expecting him… there was just something about him. Whatever it was, her own need identified with the stranger at the gate and she set off to get him a drink.

"Please… bring me a little bread as well."

She couldn't believe her ears.

Is he so blind that he cannot see I'm starving too?

Turning again to face the stranger, she let it all spill out, giving voice to the desperation of her own situation.

"As the Lord your God lives, I don't have any bread. All I have left is a handful of flour at the bottom of the bin and a drop of oil in the jug. I'm out here gathering sticks so that I can cook one last loaf for my son before we both die!"

The stranger's voice softened as he replied. It had been a long time since she had heard someone speak so tenderly to her; yet his words made no sense.

"Don't be afraid," he said. "Go ahead: bake your bread and give me the first little loaf. There will still be enough left for you and your son, for the Lord God of Israel has promised that there will always be enough flour and oil left to feed us until the famine is over, and the rain falls once more."

Never before had she heard such a thing, yet over the years she had heard rumours of Yahweh, the God of Israel. He was the God who didn't like rival gods; who had parted the Red Sea when he delivered the Israelites from slavery in Egypt. There were so many stories, but what she liked best about Yahweh was that he had given instructions on how to care for widows and provide for the poor. He could teach Baal a thing or two, as far as that was concerned, she thought. But surely this God of Israel didn't care for *her*? He couldn't possibly know her name, or even know that she existed. Yahweh was the God of Israel, not of Sidon.

Shrugging her shoulders, and with the slightest tinge of excitement rising in her heart, she decided that she had nothing to lose. Quickly picking up whatever sticks she could find, she headed off home to do as the stranger had asked. Baal had never promised her anything before; but now the Lord God of Israel had said that neither she nor her son would die… Surely that was worth taking a risk for.

Her hands were shaking as she kneaded the dough. There seemed to be so little. How could it feed all three of them? The smell of bread cooking caused a stirring under the rags once more.

"Mama, can I have some bread, please?"

The pleading, hungry eyes of her only son made her waver for a second, but something inside was calling her to do as the stranger had said.

"Soon, little one, soon. I must first feed the stranger at the gate; then I will make bread for us."

He was too weak to argue, causing her to groan at the thought that perhaps a stranger might eat what was meant for him. She had used the last of the flour and oil. Would the God of Israel really come through for her now?

The man looked very grateful as she placed the bread in his hands. She could hear him thank his God for the food before he put it to his mouth, but she didn't wait to hear what he was saying. Her feet moved faster than she thought they could as she ran back to her one little room that she called home. Holding the grain barrel in her hands, she started to shake it, her eyes tightly closed. She was afraid to look. It didn't feel any heavier, but as she shook it caused something to move in the bottom of the barrel. As she opened her eyes a tear dropped down into the barrel, creating the most beautiful little flour dust cloud she had ever seen! It was true… just as the stranger had said. The Lord God of Israel was a god who kept his word. Never did bread taste so good!

The neighbours wondered what the widow of Zarephath had to laugh about that night!

Sleep came easier when hunger pangs weren't disturbing her rest. Now, lying in the early morning light, holding her son closely for warmth, the widow was feeling the first glimmers of hope in a long time. The barrel and the jug sat in their usual place in a recess in the wall, calling her to check to see if the promise was as true on this new day as it had been the day before. Her heart was beating loudly with both excitement and fear. Excitement that it could be true… Yahweh really was a God of miracles. Fear, that she could be disappointed as she had been by so many gods before. Hearing a stirring noise from the little room her husband had built on the roof of their house, she knew that the stranger was awake and that she needed to rise to fix breakfast.

Breakfast. What a beautiful word! This time she lifted the barrel with her eyes open; a little voice within assuring her that the promise would stand. And there it was… flour… not a barrelful, but enough for breakfast! The boy couldn't believe that they were going to eat on two days in a row. His mother told him for the first time that there was a God in Israel who had promised that they would live and not die.

"What about Baal, Mama?" the little boy whispered, puzzled, his eyes fixed on the statue sitting on the shelf above his bed.

Hurriedly she covered the statue with a piece of cloth, hiding it from view: "Baal has shown us no help. We will hear what the man from Israel says about his god."

It didn't take long for the stranger to tell them stories of Yahweh. He explained that the Living God was not fashioned by man's hands, and although you couldn't see him, you could see his handiwork. He told them the story of Israel's wanderings; of the many times their sin had angered God, causing his judgment to come. The widow learnt that God always did what he said. Every day she discovered it was true, as she went to the barrel and jug; every day she was able to make food for her household.

Elijah – for that was his name – kept himself to himself, treating her with respect. He didn't go out in public very often, choosing to pray frequently in the little room on the roof of her house. There were times when he mended some things for her, but what delighted her most was to hear her son laugh as Elijah told him stories of the great adventures of the Children of Israel. They cheered and whooped together when the giant Goliath fell after the young David had downed him with a slingshot; and sat goggle-eyed at the descriptions of all the animals queuing up to get on board Noah's ark. They were the times she smiled, and the times she missed her husband the most, wishing that he too could experience the change in their home since they began to hear of the God of Israel.

Every day they were becoming stronger. Every day, she went to the barrel and jug, and every day there was enough. At first she was tentative as she gazed into the barrel, wondering how long this would go on for, but soon trusting became as natural as breathing. Her little boy started to grow in height and strength, eventually able to help with a few chores. Running errands for the neighbours brought small rewards of other daily necessities; soon he was feeling like the man of the house. One day, when he was older, he would be able to support his mother the way a son should; and make his father proud.

"Time for breakfast, little one!" she called across the room one morning.

When there was no reply from below the quilt that she had made from the rags, she set to other forms of waking him. Just like many other little boys, he felt that morning always came too early. Leaning over him, she pulled back the cover and pounced, tickling him and laughing: "Get up, sleepyhead. Can't you smell breakfast?" Pulling back in shock, she immediately saw that something was wrong. His skin felt hot, and his body lay limp against hers as she tried to waken him. The boy barely stirred, except to release a moan from his dry lips. Rushing to the water jar, she poured a little drink for him and then wet a cloth to try and cool him down. Panic was rising; her palms were sweaty, and her heart pounding in her chest.

You can't be sick, little one; I love you and need you so.

Breathing deeply, she tried to control the emotions that

were overwhelming her… emotions that were taking her back to that fateful day her husband wouldn't wake up.

"It started just like this… exactly like this," she whispered to herself, rocking the boy in her arms.

She stayed in the same position for hours; just rocking him and singing softly all the little songs he had loved when he was even littler than he was now. Helplessness entered her world once more, only this time she felt that no one could help her. He was her world… her reason for being; all she had left of her darling husband. A large, hot tear dropped on his forehead as she tried to imagine life without him, the joy of her heart. He was the sunshine in her drab existence; the reason to get up every day.

She was a mother, just like any other, who loved her child more deeply than they could ever imagine… whose heart would never only belong to herself, once that tiny baby is placed in her arms.

The hours simply rolled into each other without her noticing the time passing. But with the passing of those hours the child grew weaker, the coaxing of his mother unable to do the only thing she longed for: to waken him from unconsciousness. The pattern of his breathing was changing, and the widow had never felt so alone… so desperate.

All this time Elijah sat in his little rooftop room, listening to a mother sing, plead and weep for help from somewhere for her child. He was a solitary man, called by God to bring his word to the Children of Israel; yet on that day the dilemma of one little boy who had nibbled his way into the prophet's soul was on his mind.

The cry of death suddenly filled the house. The widow howled as grief and disaster filled her soul and her home. The boy was dead! Her crying echoed up and down the tightly packed alleys of Zarephath. Elijah ran down the crude steps leading from the roof and into the living space. In front of him was the saddest scene he had ever witnessed.

She had sunk to her knees on the dirt floor, unable to stand any longer with the weight of the child in her arms and the weight of grief in her heart. Utterly broken, she wept, swaying as she did so, holding tightly to her only darling little boy; the harrowing noise of her grief piercing the soul of the hearers. Elijah stood there, his own heart deeply touched by the scene playing out before him.

Suddenly, she noticed him standing there. Rising to face him, her countenance blackened with anger and accusation.

"What are you really doing here… you… man of God? Look, my son is dead – is that what you wanted, all along?"

The words poured from her lips in her need to blame someone for the tragedy that had just occurred.

"Did you come here just to show me how sinful I am?" she continued, "and then to punish me for my sin? Is that what this is all about?"

Before she could say any more, the same man who had bravely faced King Ahab spoke with a tenderness that he probably didn't know he possessed. No clever comments; no pointing finger; no accusations; he simply said to this devastated mother: "Give me your son," and reached out his arms towards her.

His quiet words settled her for a moment, giving her that split second to think. *This man's words gave us life before*, she thought, as she looked at the barrel and jug on the shelf in the corner. Then a little prompting from deep inside said: "Do as he says."

Quietly, she put the most precious possession she had into the arms of the stranger, and she sank back down onto the floor. Elijah rushed up the stairs to his room with the dead child held close to his chest. Never before had he held such a precious cargo in his arms.

Sitting on the floor in the room below, the widow quietly rocked, her arms empty. She could hear Elijah speaking, but the thickness of the roof prevented her from making out his words. He sounded angry, or perhaps distressed; she couldn't decide which. It made her nervous. She didn't want him to make his God angry; she had heard what could happen when God was displeased with his people. Yet Yahweh had the power to perform miracles. The barrel and the jug had taught her that. And, unbelievably, there was a strange sense of peace around her since Elijah had taken her son to the upper room.

Breaking away from her thoughts, she noticed the silence, then the sound of steps crossing the roof. She held her hand across her mouth and waited. Terror, fear and a strange excitement vied for room in her heart.

The door opened and Elijah returned. He was still carrying the boy, but now a huge smile crossed his face. The child's head was resting against his chest… no longer hanging over his arm. She was frozen to the spot.

"Look, your son is alive!" said the prophet, handing the boy back into her embrace.

Laughter and tears mingled together as they danced

around the small room. Joy and delight dethroned sorrow, as the little boy hugged his mama, declaring, "I'm hungry; have I missed breakfast?"

"In a minute, little one, in a minute," she replied, wiping her tears with her skirts. Then she placed him back on his bed, and took Elijah's hands in hers. "Now I know that you really are a man of God; and that the words that you speak are from the Lord, and that his words are always true!" And deep inside her soul, she felt that the God of heaven was pleased with her declaration of faith in him, as she felt his peace wash over her soul.

"Now," she said to Elijah, "I have breakfast to make for two hungry men!"

And laughter filled the room.

There were no more visits to the Baal shrine for the woman or her son. Day by day, she learnt more about the one true and living God from Elijah. His presence and power didn't stop at the borders of Samaria eighty miles away, nor did he only care for those within its boundaries. As the woman listened to Elijah tell of how he came to be in Zarephath, she realized that the God of heaven must have known her name to send him to her house. She may have been poor and widowed, rejected as unimportant by the people of her town because she had no husband, but she knew she was not invisible to God. And she also knew without a shadow of a doubt that the God who knew her name, loved her deeply – deeply enough to show his kindness to a pagan woman in a foreign land. For that he would always have her heart.

Almost two years had passed since she had met the stranger at the gate, and one morning Elijah brought his walking staff down to breakfast with him. Looking at the gnarled piece of wood staring at her from the corner, she knew what was coming.

"It's time," he said. "Time to go to see Ahab again."

The widow was about to protest when Elijah put his hand up to stop her.

"I told you that this day would come. God has spoken, and I am his servant."

She served slowly, trying to stall the inevitable; yet there was impatience in Elijah that told her of his desire to obey quickly. Sadly, she filled his little leather bag with what she could spare for his journey. Eighty miles was a long walk.

For those two years he had lodged at her house, and in one sense he was no longer a stranger. Her life and her home had been changed during that time – changed for the better. She knew that she and her son would miss him, but as he walked through the city gate for the last time she was not afraid, for the Lord God of Israel had not left with him. She had experienced Yahweh as the living God, and he lived in Zarephath as well as Israel. Of that she was sure.

And Elijah didn't stop to look back as they watched his figure fade into the distance.

AD 1987

Centuries later, and hundreds of miles from Sarafand (present day Zarephath), also living in a seaside town, was another woman to whom life had not been kind. Although this woman's husband was alive and well, their marriage was strained by their difficult daily circumstances. They too had only one child, a daughter.

"Are you sure you can manage?" the woman asked, pushing her arm into the sleeve of her coat. "I don't have to go, you know. In fact I don't want to go; I'd be happy to have an excuse; just say the word."

"Go," replied her tired-looking husband. "When was the last time you were out for the evening? I'll manage fine."

"You could hardly call going to a church meeting a night out, now, could you?" A sarcastic smile crossed her face as she finished buttoning her coat. "It's just that I've said 'No' to Joan so many times that I thought if I went this once she'd get off my back and leave me alone. Poor thing thinks that this woman who's speaking tonight might be able to help me. Help? The last thing we need is help from church… much good it's done us up to now."

"She's only trying to be kind. Please, love, behave yourself… and try to enjoy it."

She tutted, and leant forward to give him a peck on the cheek, but a grunting noise from the corner of the room stopped her mid-kiss. Struggling to remove her coat again, she knelt on the floor beside her little girl, whose limbs had stiffened and were shaking in a seizure. Gently turning her slightly on to her side, they watched, helpless as always to do anything but wait until the ravaging of her body stilled once more. Wiping the foam from the side of her mouth to ease the passage of air through her clenched jaw, the parents looked at each other in despair.

"I'm staying home," she said. "I can't leave her like this."

The noisy breathing ceased and the child wriggled, moaning as she did so.

"There, sweetheart; it's all over," she said, slipping her arms gently under the child's slight body and scooping her on to her knee. The little girl blinked and a hint of a smile crossed her beautiful face. Smoothing the kink in her lovely red hair, the mother sighed, cuddling her precious child close.

"You're going," said a firm voice from the kitchen. "I'll give her her medicine now and that will settle her. Tonight is no different from any other. Trust me; I can manage."

As he appeared, brown glass bottle in hand, the woman sighed in her husband's direction. He was right. Tonight was no different from any other. The little girl's seizures were a devastating part of her condition, caused by a brain disorder. For years now every kind of medicine had been tried, but none of them could stop the distressing seizures that tormented their lovely daughter. At best they were controlled for a few hours. But it was the nights that were the worst. How she dreaded the nights.

The noise of tooting from a car horn outside made the little girl smile, pulling her mother away from her thoughts.

"OK, OK, I'm coming," she said, gently returning the child to her cosy cushions on the settee. Kissing them both, she left father and daughter to the evening bedtime routine, rushing outside coat in hand.

The coastal drive was breathtaking as I approached the seaside town where I was due to speak that evening. The azure blue sea may have looked like the Mediterranean, but there would be no swimmers in its freezing waters. A few small fishing boats were already making their way out of the harbour; anxious to land a big enough catch to pay the bills and keep food on the table for their families. It was a difficult life, and many in this area of Ireland had followed the family tradition of fishing for a livelihood. As a city girl I was filled with admiration for the fishermen; any sense of romance I felt quickly dispersed as I watched the boats sail away into the distance.

The church hall was already buzzing when I arrived. The ladies had been working hard for this special event, and thankfully it was paying off, as women streamed in to take their seats. The supper tables around the walls were bedecked with flowers, making an austere building welcoming and colourful. There's something lovely about the happy chat of women who have escaped the pressure of domesticity for a short time. It has such an air of relaxation and anticipation.

By the time the meeting was ready to start, the large room was well filled; only a few empty seats remaining at the front. I had been ushered up to the platform with the rest of those taking part, feeling rather conspicuous sitting in full view of all present. However, it always amazes me how much you can see when in front of an audience. There's the last-minute dash to turn off the mobile phone, or the bag of sweets passed down the row; or those who are desperately trying to fit in a month's conversation with a friend before the proceedings begin. Then there are the faces… all kinds of people from differing life situations. And I often wonder why they have come and what are the dreams and longings of their hearts.

It was as I was looking around and soaking up the atmosphere that I first noticed one lady in particular. She looked uncomfortable and embarrassed, as her friend rushed her to the front seats just as the meeting began. Her friend sang with great gusto, while she merely mumbled into the hymn sheet. I groaned inwardly, wishing that they didn't insist on singing hymns at these events, making the visitors feel even more like outsiders. As the minutes rolled past, I had to correct myself for looking at her so often. But she looked so sad, so tired. The impression portrayed was one of attendance under duress; longing to be somewhere else, rather than this environment that seemed so foreign to her.

The soloist soon had the ladies eating out of her hand; the words and music filling the room with the reality of God's help through heartache. Except for the lady on the front row. Her face was now red, her eyes firmly fixed on the floor, her arms tightly folded against her chest.

She looked furious.

As I went to the podium to speak, I wondered what was making this lady so angry. I didn't have long to wait for the answer – only the length of my talk. I'd spent forty minutes speaking from my heart of how, as a young mother, I had discovered that our first child was born with a genetic condition that had left her profoundly disabled. I told them honestly and openly how angry I had been with God; totally unable to understand how God could allow this in my life and afraid of what lay ahead for us as a family. Unfolding my own journey with God towards acceptance and peace, I explained emotionally the detour my healing had taken when our third child, at this time still a baby, was born with the same condition as her older sister. I could see all over the room that I wasn't the only woman there who had suffered disappointment or tragedy. Yet my desire that night was not to leave them merely with a sad story, but rather to tell them how God was helping me to face each and every day with his presence and his promises in my life. The God of heaven, I believed, was able to help in every single situation of life.

The clatter of cups brought pleasant relief from what was probably a difficult meeting for some of those present. When my hostess left an empty seat beside me to check up on things in the kitchen, I noticed out of the corner of my eye the "angry" lady being manhandled towards me by her well-meaning friend. I gulped and prayed a quick: "Help, Lord!"

Pleasantries didn't last too long, as the lady got straight to it, giving an explanation of the picture of anger that she had displayed throughout the meeting. She told me of her beautiful, redheaded daughter at home. She was twelve now; severely disabled, tormented by seizures. So badly was the child affected that she had to sleep in her bed, between her and her husband. It was obvious that the poor woman hated the night time; dreaded it, in fact. At times it seemed that she hadn't been listening to me at all; hadn't heard that my daughter also had seizures and that I knew just how she felt. But her pain was so acute that she didn't believe anyone could know what she was going through. Her heartache was isolating; or perhaps it was the wall that she had built around herself that was the truly isolating object in her life. A wall of anger and bitterness, cemented together by heartache and sorrow – this was a wall I simply couldn't scale.

So I let her rant and complain, recognizing that I could so easily be standing in her shoes. Platitudes were not what she needed, so I said little. My heart sank, however, when she said with all the conviction she could muster: "Don't speak to me about God! He doesn't even know I exist! You may think he's interested in you, but he doesn't even know my name! Not once… not even once has he ever answered *my* prayers… for *my* child. He doesn't know me and I don't want to know him!"

By now the ladies sitting around us had gone quiet, as her voice was raised, her friend trying to persuade her to leave before she created even more of a scene. As she walked away, angrily shrugging off her friend's hand from her shoulder, my heart broke for her. Even though she wouldn't believe it, I too knew the kind of pain she was experiencing: a mother's pain for her suffering child.

The long journey home was so different from the one I had made earlier. The lightness of my mood had been replaced by a deep sadness. Sadness for this lady who cared for a needy, sick child every day, with no hope for the future and no help for today. She was miserable, angry, lonely and desperately disappointed with God. I felt that I had failed her… failed to help her realize that God *did* know her name and cared for her more deeply than she could ever imagine. As tears dripped onto my lap, I did the only thing I could for her: I prayed... prayed that God would reveal himself to this nameless woman with the broken heart.

Nine months had passed, and spring was just around the corner. It had been a difficult winter, with our eldest daughter's health problems taking a dip into the dangerous. Still, she was holding on, surprising the doctors by her tenacious grip on life.

One morning, having just completed her little sister's physiotherapy routine, I heard the click of the letterbox.

"Ah, Joy, it's the postman," I said, tickling her tummy as I went to the hall to collect the mail. Only one of the letters was exclusively for me, and the postmark got me wondering who could be writing to me from there? It was a letter from the minister's wife of the church on the coast.

"Do you remember," she inquired, "the lady who was so cross with you at our spring event?"

What a silly question, I thought; *that's one lady I'll never forget!*

"Well, she's asked me to write to you," she continued. "In fact her very words were: 'Tell that woman, who spoke that night, that I know now that God knows my name; and that I've asked him to be my saviour.'"

I didn't know whether to laugh or cry; my heart felt as if it was bursting as I read the rest of the story.

The minister's wife went on to tell how the woman's plight had deeply touched a few of her ladies, who then started to build a bridge of little kindnesses to her heart. Simple small things at first… an apple tart or a pot of soup; perhaps a pile of laundry ironed when her daughter was ill, or a bit of weeding done to pretty up her garden. Eventually, she had trusted a few of them to babysit, enabling her and her husband to have their first night out together in years. Slowly, brick by brick, the wall of bitterness began to be dismantled, until one day she turned up at church with her husband and their little girl. Now surrounded by a small group of people who really cared for her, she began to see that it was God who had put her on their hearts. Perhaps he did care for her after all.

She finished her long, beautiful letter by telling me how one day the lady asked her if she remembered the bit from the Bible I had mentioned that night. It was from Isaiah 43, and as the minister's wife read her the first two verses: "Fear not, for I have redeemed you; I have called you by your name; you are mine. When you pass through the waters, I will be with you," the lady stopped her.

"I want Jesus to be my saviour. That woman was right… he does know my name, and I want him to be with me the way he was with her."

The angels were not the only ones rejoicing at that news!

Almost a year later, I received another letter. This time it came from the lady herself. It was short and to the point. She wanted me to know that her beautiful little redhead was for ever free from her dreaded seizures. She had died just the week before; now God was walking through the "waters" with her and her husband. They were not alone.

As I held her letter in my hand, I wept for her loss, rejoiced for the hope she now had in heaven because of Jesus and thrilled at the thought of a God who knows our name and acts on our behalf... whatever the century... whatever the location... whatever the situation.

About "Nameless"

C. 865 BC

Read for yourself the biblical account of the story of the widow of Zarephath in the Old Testament book of 1 Kings 17:8 – 18:1.

AD 1987

This is the true story of an encounter between the author and the people mentioned in the chapter.

Hopeless

C. AD 31

"Reuben, what are you doing? You don't have enough food with you to feed a sparrow," she said, sighing and snatching the worn leather bag from his grasp. "It will be sundown before you return, and the work will be heavy: first day of harvest is always the busiest. Let me pack more bread and cheese for you."

"Stop fussing, woman; I have enough!" His reply was gruff as he retrieved the bag. As he did so their hands touched and, catching her glance, he saw sadness in her dark eyes. "I am sorry, Deborah," he said, quietening his tone. "I didn't mean to shout; we will talk later. I have a lot on my mind." Turning to leave the room, he spoke, trying to ease the tension between them: "You and Caleb are coming by the olive grove later, aren't you?"

"Yes. Caleb has chosen a big stick to shake down as many olives as he can. He wants to show his papa what a big boy he is now."

Her chin trembled as she spoke, allowing her husband a peek beyond the guard she was constructing around her heart; one that she hoped was strong enough for whatever was coming. For weeks now her handsome, hard-working husband had barely touched her. Every day he worked in his little potter's shed from early morning until late into the night. What was she doing wrong? Why did he not want to spend time alone with her? Could it be that her worst nightmare was coming true… that he didn't love her any more?

Reuben tipped his head to clear the lintel of the door, all he needed for the day strapped onto his back. He didn't look back at the lonely figure of his lovely wife standing in front of the house in case she would see the rogue tear running down his weather-beaten cheek to hide in his beard. Soon he would have to tell her; he wouldn't be able to keep it to himself for much longer. And the picture in her eyes this morning told him that he was breaking her heart, even now. The chill of the early autumn made him shiver, but not as much as the secret that was isolating him from those he loved. A huge sigh caused a vapour cloud to rise into the air.

I do love you, my dear, sweet Deborah, I really do.

"Papa, Papa!" came a sound that jolted him back from his private thoughts.

As he turned quickly, the picture of his only daughter running down the stony path stopped him in his tracks and melted his heart. The early morning sunshine glinted in her long wavy hair, bouncing on her shoulders as she ran.

"Papa, you left without kissing me goodbye," she shouted, jumping into his arms.

"You are getting too old for your papa's kisses," he teased, burying his face in her hair.

"Never! I'll never be too old for my papa's kisses!"

"OK, then. Right here," he said, pointing.

Planting a noisy smacker of a kiss on his cheek, she giggled as he set her feet back on the ground.

"Now, Sarah, my princess, run home to help your mother. She'll be wondering where you have gone; and remember, I want plenty of water ready for me when I get home… there'll be pots to make, olive harvest or not."

For the first time in a long while, a smile crossed his face as he watched the girl skip back through the alleys of the small town that had been his family home for years. God had been good in giving him such a beautiful daughter, and a son; every man is especially blessed when he has a son, and one day Caleb would take over as head of the family… one day.

By the time he was passing through the city gates, others had joined him, their conversation turning his mind to the job in hand. It was olive harvest, and as the men walked towards the olive grove the mood was upbeat. The previous year's harvest had been poor, as was common with this fruit… bumper crops every other year, that was the norm, and this year looked like being an exceptional yield. That also made Reuben smile; he needed a good crop, this year especially.

"Reuben!" a familiar voice called to him from the area of the grove that was planted with their trees. "Come on, brother, or the day will be half over before you begin! What happened? Did the lovely Deborah keep you back this morning, eh?"

Reuben tried to ignore the taunts of the family joker and, after bidding his brother Josh a good morning, he set to work. Josh had already spread an oiled cloth under part of the tree, pegging it firmly to the ground. Reuben covered the remaining ground with the cloth he had carried in his backpack. By the time he stood back to take a good look at the tree planted by his grandfather years earlier, Josh was balancing on one of the branches.

"Yahweh must have a sense of humour, don't you think, Reuben?"

"What are you talking about, Josh?" Reuben replied, arming himself with a short, thick piece of wood.

"Well, look at this tree. Did you ever see anything as ugly as the olive tree? Yet it produces a fruit that feeds us, and an oil that can give us light in the darkness, treat our ailments, shine our furniture and even make our wives more beautiful?"

"Enough talking, brother, and get down from there, for when I hit this trunk your bones will shake like the branches."

As Reuben swung the stick towards the gnarled trunk of the old tree, his young brother jumped clear. Soon the olives were falling like hail from the sky into the cloth below. Each blow brought more reward for their labour, filling Reuben with a deep satisfaction that at least this part of his plan was coming together. Blow after hefty blow rained down on the bruised tree trunk as the morning progressed.

"Enough, Reuben, enough." Josh caught his brother's arm before he could land another blow. "This old bird's not going to give us any more without a fight. Remember the law, Reuben: leave what clings to the branches for the poor to gather… who knows? We could be like them, some day."

"I have a family to provide for, brother… they come first."

"Of course they do, but we have five other heavily laden trees to harvest. Leave it, and gather up what we have for the olive press. What's wrong with you, Reuben? You aren't normally the selfish type!"

Reuben winced at these wounding words, his silence

speaking louder than any reply could. Josh was right. He was too intense, and it was showing in a selfishness that was alien to the big-hearted Jew. Perhaps if he shared what was on his heart with his little brother, then he would understand? But no, he must speak to Deborah first… he owed her that much.

The greenish-grey foliage provided excellent protection from the sun as they pegged the cloths below the second tree. Josh, never usually without a word, was working quietly, watching the man he had idolized since before he could say even his name. Memories of boyhood play danced in his mind, but something wasn't right, and he determined to get it out of him before they finished for the day.

"Papa, Papa, I'm here!" came the excited call of a little boy making his way through the trees, wielding a stick almost as big as himself.

Ripples of laughter followed him through the grove as the men watched him ducking around one tree after another in his attempt to find his father. The little man with the big stick was a tender yet funny sight.

"Over here, Caleb," boomed his father's voice, giving some direction to the boy's search.

Both men moved towards the child with obvious affection, swinging him round and around between the trees, to whoops of delight. As they set him to the ground he stumbled, dizzy from the spinning.

"It's good to see you smile, Reuben. At least your son still brings you joy."

Sensing the sarcasm in her voice, Josh greeted his sister-in-law with a kiss and grabbed Caleb's hand: "OK, Caleb, let's see just how strong you are. We have olives to fell!"

"Deborah, I didn't see you coming," Reuben replied awkwardly, trying to make small talk as Deborah poured some wine from the skin she had brought with her. They ate their lunch under the shade of the third tree, resting for a time in the heat of the day. Reuben groaned as Josh woke him from his nap, realizing that he had slept through most of Deborah and Caleb's visit.

"Caleb wanted to waken you to show you how many olives he had gathered, but Deborah wouldn't let him. He was so excited: his first olive harvest… and you missed it!"

Josh lifted his stick, his fist tightening around it. For a moment Reuben wondered whether his little brother was tempted to use it on him rather than the tree.

"I don't know what's going on, Reuben, but you need to sort it – and soon!"

As the day started to cool, Reuben didn't know whether the poorer olive crop from the third tree was due to his exhaustion and aching muscles or the deep pain in his heart. His life was about to fall apart and he knew that no one could stop it. The two brothers headed home in silence. One more day should finish the olive gathering.

The basin and cloth sat perched on the tripod as Reuben walked into the small garden that surrounded his house. Stopping for a moment to wash, his senses were hit by the smell of lentil stew wafting out of the house to meet him. Unusually, he wasn't hungry. It was dusk, and the place was strangely quiet: a soft, snoring sound coming from the corner of the room as he entered.

"He couldn't stay awake a minute longer," Deborah whispered, running her fingers through her hair. "All the excitement of the day got the better of him."

Without warning, the silence was broken by the sound of sloshing water, as Sarah rushed into the room, precariously carrying a basin.

"Papa, you're home. I have some water to wash your poor tired and dusty feet."

Before Reuben could reply, Sarah had pushed him into the chair and was pulling off his sandals.

"No Sarah – you mustn't!"

The panic in her father's voice frightened the child and she fell back onto the floor, crying. But it was too late.

"Your foot, Papa… what is wrong with your foot?"

Deborah gasped, shocked at the sight before her. The side of Reuben's foot was angry and raw; a huge ulcer had eaten a hole in his flesh.

"Reuben, what is it? What's wrong?"

"It's just a cut," he replied, nodding frantically toward Sarah.

Realizing that he didn't want to talk in front of the child, Deborah gained her composure quickly, helping Sarah up from the floor.

"You heard Papa… it's just a cut. Come now and help Mama put out the stew. Papa has worked hard today, and us women have to make sure our men get a good meal."

Quickly covering the wound with an old piece of rag, Reuben slipped his sandals back on to his feet. His hand shook as he leaned forward to take the bowl of stew offered by Sarah.

The child's expression hadn't altered during the time her mother had tried to occupy her with serving. Fear had expelled the light in her eyes, and a little sob escaped as she turned to the cooking pot once more.

Only the sound of spoons scraping against bowls broke the uncomfortable silence. Each of them struggled to eat; no one wanted a second helping.

Reuben lifted Sarah on to his knee and held her close.

"Don't fret, Princess," he said, planting a gentle kiss on her head. "Papa will be fine, you'll see."

Breaking away from his embrace, she ran into her mother's arms. For the first time ever, she had heard her father lie.

"I'm going to my wheel," he said, rising from the table and casting a look of despair over the pathetic scene unfolding before him. Deborah was rubbing Sarah's back, rocking to and fro, and trying to calm the child. Their eyes met as he rose to leave... but whose contained the most pain was hard to tell.

A tear rolled off the end of his nose and caused a little ripple on the surface of the water as Reuben moved the bucket towards the potter's wheel.

She's such a clever child; I'm sure she knows... Deborah will definitely have guessed... we must talk tonight... there are so many things I need to explain to her before I leave.

Silent conversation filled his head and tormented his heart. The tears flowed faster; tears that until now had been held back by a dam of resolve – a resolve to put as much in place as possible for his precious family before he wasn't allowed to stay with them any longer. But as he fiercely pounded clay against wood, the hopelessness of his situation overwhelmed him. What could he do? It was so unfair. No one could help him. Fate had dealt him the most vicious of blows. He felt condemned, alone and unclean.

The minutes passed into hours, as his feet paddled on and on, the wheel turning faster and faster, clay bowls piling up around him as he worked on like a man possessed.

"Reuben! Reuben… Reuben."

He could hear a voice, as if in the distance; a voice that he recognized – that he loved. But he couldn't stop. He had so little time now. He had to keep going. More pots meant more money for Deborah and the children. *Deborah*. That's whose voice he heard; but he must keep going.

"Reuben… stop! Please stop – you are exhausted!"

The clay shot around the room, sticking to the walls as his hands were pulled away from the wheel.

"Reuben… stop, please! Sarah is finally asleep. We must talk!"

Holding his clay-covered hands in hers, Deborah looked into his eyes and saw the brokenness in the man she had loved since her father told her that Reuben's father had agreed to their betrothal.

"It's a good match, Deborah. He's a good man – he will look after you."

His words echoed in her memory as they stared at each other in silence, and after all these years those words were still true.

"Why didn't you tell me, Reuben?" she asked, stroking his face gently. "I thought I had done something wrong – thought you didn't love me any more. Why? Why?"

"I needed to prepare; needed to get as much gathered together as possible for you and the children before I go to the priest. You'll be able to keep going for quite a while, selling these pots… and then there's the olive harvest. It's a good one this year, Deborah – it'll pay the Roman taxes and leave something for you to live on."

"The priest? You really think that it's… it's… ?"

"Leprosy. It's leprosy, Deborah. Why do you think I've tried to stay away from you? I love you… so much, but I can't risk you becoming ill too. The children need you."

Reuben stepped away from her and pulled back the hair covering his right ear. Deborah gasped, as the sore became visible.

"I can't hide it any longer. Just let me finish the olive harvest tomorrow and then I'll show myself to the priest. One more day, Deborah… just one more day."

The silence spoke louder than their words as they lay together for what was left of the night. Reuben had tried to keep his distance from Deborah, wanting to protect her from this dreadful illness, but her cries of "just one more night" ate away at his heart, and he wrapped himself around her for the last time.

As the sunbeams peeked through the cracks of the one little window in their home, Reuben tried to store in his memory how every nook and cranny looked. The sight of his darling children slumbering as dawn broke caused a choking noise to escape from his dry throat. Panic suddenly enveloped him. He would miss them growing up… miss Sarah's wedding… miss teaching Caleb how to throw a pot. He couldn't bear to think what the realization of his fears meant. As his thoughts ran riot, sobs escaped against his will. The heaving of his chest caused Deborah to stir, and he desperately tried to hold back the pain as his life fell apart.

It should all have been so different. They should have spent many years together enjoying their simple, hard-working life. Now the future was bleak; no – the future was unimaginable. No one could help him. Even the Lord Jehovah had forsaken him.

Without a word, Deborah held him close, feeling his warm tears running down her neck. Hearing a yawn from the corner, Reuben tried to compose himself. The children mustn't see him like this.

"Remember all I told you," he whispered, "and never forget that I love you – whatever happens."

Soon Caleb was jumping all over him, shouting about his victories over the olive tree. Meanwhile, Sarah turned her face towards the wall, struggling with her thoughts of the night before. Once the early morning routine was complete and Reuben's bag was packed for the last day in the olive grove, he set his precious family around him. Brave words found their way from his lips as he spoke of the Law of Moses, and how the Lord Jehovah had given instructions on how the Children of Israel should live in order that sickness would not destroy their people. Sarah quietly sobbed as her papa continued. Caleb listened wide-eyed, sensing nothing unusual in this conversation, as his papa often spoke of the Law and the Prophets before he would help his papa recite the Shema each morning and evening. However, his young brow furrowed as he listened to the strength of his life say that he had to show himself to the priest today, and that he might not be able to come home for a long time.

He felt his mama's arms tighten around him as the realization hit home. Papa was going to leave them… he was sick… he might not come back!

"No, Papa! No!"

"Caleb, I need you to be strong. You will be the man of the house now. Uncle Josh will help you. Perhaps I can come home soon. Until then, I want you to recite the Shema every day for your mama and Sarah, that the Lord may bless this house."

The child's sobbing broke Reuben's heart. He felt a failure as a father. How could he fulfil the Shema? Wasn't he supposed to be the one to "teach his children God's commands… sitting in their home… walking by the road"?

"Come, Caleb, it's time – dry your tears."

Reuben's strong voice had a power about it that surprised even him. Deborah stood bravely with Sarah as the two men in her life, standing side by side, declared their belief in a God who had been faithful to his people for generations. Her heart, although breaking, was filled with pride as they affirmed:

"Hear, O Israel: The Lord our God, the Lord is one! You shall love the Lord your God with all your heart, with all your soul, and with all your strength."

And as she listened to her brave husband's voice booming through their little home, Deborah was warmed by a strange sense of a presence that she had never felt before.

She held the children close into her skirts, trying to muffle their cries as the love of her life walked out through the door, perhaps for the last time. Only when she thought he was out of earshot did she allow herself to wail in the desperation that was consuming her.

Reuben's gaze was fixed on the path ahead as he walked towards the olive grove. Greeting Josh with an anxious look, the young man knew that something terrible was about to break, but they worked on in silence; at twice the speed of any of the others around them. There was no time for jokes or casual conversation; only the promise that they would talk as soon as the last three trees were harvested. So Josh waited.

True to his word, Reuben sat under the shade of the last olive tree as the sun was at its highest. Josh didn't interrupt his elder brother as he unburdened his soul. Tears washed little tracks down his dusty weather-beaten face. For once in his young life he had nothing to say. Both of the men had seen it happen in the lives of others, men, women, children; this disease was no respecter of age or sex. Some disappeared, never to be seen again; others only had to go away for a week or two. It all depended on the priest: he it was who made the decision as to whether or not the lesions on the skin were true leprosy or not.

"It'll only be for a few weeks Reuben, you'll see," were the only words of encouragement Josh could manage.

Reuben's silent shake of the head said differently, as he went on to explain to his brother all he had left in place to provide for his family for as long as possible.

Josh promised that he would do all he could for them, and Reuben rose to leave. They lingered for a short while in a strong brotherly embrace, each feeling the thud of the other's heart. Then Reuben picked up his bag and walked away.

"Shalom, Deborah."

Deborah put down her cleaning cloth at the sound of the greeting outside her home. This was one visit she had been expecting, and yet it also signalled that her fears had been realized. Sarah and Caleb ran to hide behind her back, every bone in her body shaking as she went to greet her visitor.

"Shalom, Deborah," he repeated, as she stood before him.

His clothing gave his identity away, but in their small community the man was well known. Introductions were not needed.

"Shalom, Rabbi," Deborah replied, her voice barely more than a squeak.

"You know why I have come. Reuben told me that he had prepared you for the sad news I must deliver to your home today. He has to go outside the city for a time – and if the sores go, we will see… we will see."

All the emotion of the previous twenty-four hours came upon her at once, and falling to the ground in great distress, she wept, holding the children so tightly that it frightened them.

The priest knew that words were of no use at this time. He had done this too many times before. It was best that he carried on with his business. How he hated this part of his job! Pushing past Deborah and the children, he went inside to check the house. If any mould was present he would have to put the family out until it could be dealt with. Oh, how he hoped that would not have to happen. Unknown to him, Deborah and the children had been cleaning and scrubbing since Reuben had left for the olive grove that morning. There wasn't a cleaner house in the whole city!

In his little eccentric way, the priest came out muttering to himself, and as his eyes met Deborah's his face lit up. "Good news, my child; the house is free from disease. You have much to be thankful for. God is good."

Biting her tongue, she bade him farewell.

Thankful? I have nothing to be thankful for – while Reuben lives with the unclean… and my children have no father, I have nothing to be thankful for!

It was a long walk to the caves from the main road. Reuben thought about how often he had passed the place where the lepers lived; rushing by, hoping he wouldn't meet any of them on the way. They were unclean; a danger to society; people to be avoided at all costs. Or that's how he had thought – until now.

Turning a bend in the dusty road, he came upon a woman who was startled to see him. Raising her hand to cover her mouth, she shouted, "Unclean!" as she tried to avoid bumping into him.

"No, stop, please!" he called after her as she tried to run away. "Can you help me? I've been sent here by the priest… I… might… have… leprosy," he stuttered.

Still holding her shawl across her mouth, she pointed in the direction of the caves behind her.

"God have mercy!" she whispered, with a look of genuine sorrow in her eyes.

Approaching the network of caves, Reuben was surprised by the number of people that he saw. Many were ragged and thin, but it was the look on their faces that distressed him the most. Men, women, boys and girls – they all looked the same: dejected. Empty eyes – despairing and without hope. Lost.

A sense of panic grabbed him. He wanted to run away from this awful place. He wanted to go home – to Deborah and the children. His chest tightened; the noise of his heart, beating faster and faster, almost deafened him. He gasped for breath, as the world around him started to spin. In the enveloping blackness he managed just one word, as his body sank powerless to the ground.

"Help!"

As he became aware of the light returning, he was choking on the water being poured down his throat. Opening his eyes, he jumped in shock at the sight of the man who had come to his aid. He tried to pull away, but the man held him tightly.

"Yes, yes, look at my face. Soon yours will be just like it. Get used to it – you're a leper too, or you wouldn't be here."

Reuben couldn't reply. His head was still spinning. It couldn't be true – he couldn't end up like this man – could he? All around him, people went about their business. A woman was helping her child to walk – but the child had only one foot. A man was struggling to carry wood – but his fingerless hands kept dropping the load. His eyes continued around what appeared to be a communal area, but there was no community... no real community. The place was filled with a strange silence. There was no exchange of conversation. No talk of the weather or of the crops; no smiling; no laughter; no singing; no children playing. Instead, the air was thick with an oppressive sadness; an indescribable loneliness; a sense of overwhelming rejection –

the rejection of both man and God.

Like the stabbing of a dagger, the sharpness of reality pierced Reuben's soul. He was no longer a man – he was a leper.

Day after weary day passed. He tried to occupy himself, but he had no tools. Even if he had his wheel, he wouldn't have been able to sell anything. Even the shadow of the leper was seen as a threat by the normal people in the world he had left behind. There were no friendships in this place, as the burden of being "unclean" became the personal identity that separated you even from those who suffered as you did.

The two follow-up visits to see the priest only confirmed his leprosy, and sank him further into despair.

The nights were the worst, when he missed the loving touch of his darling wife and the security of his own home. He discovered that suffering can turn men into something other than they were. And so Reuben literally slept on what very few belongings he had, as things had the habit of "disappearing" into the darkness. And it wasn't only "things" that could disappear in the night. He woke once just in time to stop a rat from finishing off what was left of his big toe. Leprosy devours your flesh, but its lack of pain is a double-edged sword when you are trying to retain your limbs.

Each morning and evening he recited the Shema quietly, while at the same time picturing his growing son doing the same thing in his place at home. How he missed the sabbath and the friendly, sometimes fierce discussions he would have with the other men at their synagogue meetings.

The book of Leviticus was the first book he had learnt as

a boy. It was the book of "And God says..." that gave direct instruction as to how they were to live. It was the book that said: *"Now the leper on whom the sore is, his clothes shall be torn and his head bare; and he shall cover his moustache, and cry, 'Unclean! Unclean!' He shall be unclean. All the days he has the sore he shall be unclean. He is unclean, and he shall dwell alone; his habitation shall be outside the camp."* It all seems so sensible; such good health advice – until, that is, you are the one who can no longer approach either God or man because *you* are the one who is unclean.

And his heart was sad at the thought of never again attending the festivals at Jerusalem; never again celebrating the deliverance of Israel by the hand of Yahweh; never again feeling clean in the eyes of his Maker.

In the early days he had an arrangement to meet Deborah regularly, not far from the city gates. She would leave food at a certain place; some oil and wine for his sores; and sometimes a new tunic for him. They would stay at a safe distance, and if the weather was calm they could shout their greetings loud enough to be heard. Occasionally she brought the children with her, but seeing their father as his disease worsened only upset them, so he asked Deborah not to bring them any more.

That day was the lowest of the low. How Reuben longed for death. He could see that worry was making Deborah old before her time. She needed to be free of him, or so he thought. And so Reuben decided to work harder at finding the different places where the poor received charity, so that she wouldn't have to come so often.

Yet in his longing to be kind, he broke her heart even more.

Day followed day, and month followed month. Seasons came and went, and all Reuben had left were memories. Yet, with the passage of time, it seemed that the good ones were becoming harder to recall. His body was ravaged by the disease that had taken him away from those he loved; the deformities now as hideous as the man he shrank from on that first day. He was slowly drowning in a sea of hopelessness, and his daily prayer was that of the forgotten.

How long, O Lord? Will you forget me forever? How long will you hide your face from me?

But Reuben was unaware that heaven had already heard his cries.

The journey to meet Deborah was particularly difficult that day. He was weak, his legs barely able to carry him. He was simply "full of leprosy" now. As he drew near to their meeting place, he saw her lovely form silhouetted against the sun. She was waving. He was too weak to wave back.

She was jumping up and down now – apparently excited about something. How good to see her look happy – it had been a long time since he had seen her smile.

"Reuben! Reuben! Come closer!" she shouted.

"I can't. You know I can't!"

His reply was difficult for her to make out, and as she moved towards him he fell backwards.

"Deborah, don't come any closer!" he shouted, with all the effort he could muster.

"Reuben, I must come close enough for you to hear. I

won't touch you, I promise, but I have wonderful news for you. I need to tell you about Jesus – Jesus of Nazareth."

Exhaustion meant that Reuben found it easier to stay on the ground as Deborah started to talk. He had never seen her so animated, so excited. At times she talked so quickly that he had to stop her, if he was going to understand anything of what she was saying. She talked of this rabbi – this teacher called Jesus – who was confounding the Pharisees; embarrassing the Sadducees; befriending the poor; teaching from the prophets like no one ever had before.

"And he performs miracles, Reuben!"

"He does what?"

"He performs miracles! He heals people!"

"That's not possible, Deborah!"

"I've seen it, Reuben – with my own eyes!" She stopped just long enough to catch her breath. "He cast out a demon from a man in the synagogue, Reuben. He healed the mother-in-law of one of his own followers. People are coming to him from everywhere – and he is healing them, Reuben... he is healing them."

And deep down in his soul Reuben remembered the end of the prayer of the forgotten that King David sang centuries before: *"But I have trusted in your mercy; my heart shall rejoice in your salvation."*

And for the first time in years he felt hope rise in his heart.

Sleep wouldn't come, as Reuben went over the things that Deborah had told him of this rabbi called Jesus. They talked until dusk; until Reuben knew for sure that this could be no ordinary man. In fact, Deborah said that many thought he might be the Messiah, the One promised from God. For four hundred years God had been silent; there was now no prophet in Israel – and yet there was that strange character roaming around telling people to repent and be baptized. What was it one of the others told him? Oh yes, the man had said, *there was one coming after him who was greater than he was.* Could that be this Jesus that Deborah spoke of?

Reuben's mind was in a whirl and he could feel his heart beating so fast that it frightened him. If only he could get to this Jesus, maybe, just maybe he would be willing to heal him. But no one knew where Jesus was going to turn up next. It seems he kept disappearing into the wilderness because the crowds never left him alone. And how would Reuben get close enough to him? He was a leper and forbidden to approach others. Yet, deep in the recesses of his heart, Reuben knew he must try. It was the only hope he had left, and what was it the rabbi had drummed into them at school?

The Lord Jehovah does not forsake His people for ever.

With the first shafts of light falling on the floor of the cave, Reuben lifted his belongings and rolled them up quietly. He had a plan.

It seemed that Jesus was visiting town after town, and if he came to their town he would have to come by the main road and through the gates. So Reuben planned to hide himself as near to the gate as possible, taking care not to be seen by those who would chase him away. It wouldn't be the first time a stone had bloodied his body when he came too close for others' comfort.

He was as nervous as a kitten as he waited, hour after hour, behind the large boulder yards away from the city gates. At times his excitement turned into despair, but the grain of hope that had been planted kept pushing away the negative thoughts that vied for his attention. The heat of the day had turned into the chill of the night. Only once had he almost been discovered, and he held his breath until he nearly passed out trying not to make a sound that would give him away. As his body shook in the cold, he longed for the return of the sun.

It was a busy road, and Reuben wondered how he would recognize Jesus. As the sun rose high in the sky, he heard yet another group of travellers pass by his hiding place. He cautiously moved to where he could see them, but it was something one of them said that made him gasp.

"But Jesus, explain to us once again what you meant about being the salt of the earth?"

"Jesus! He's here!" Reuben whispered to himself as excitement, panic and fear all took hold of him at once. In the seconds he took to regain his composure, the little band of men had already passed through the gate.

It was now or never. Habit forced him to cover his mouth as he ran after Jesus.

"Unclean! Unclean!" he shouted at the trader as he rushed past him.

Suddenly there was some panic, as people saw the leper enter the city, and the noise behind them stopped Jesus and his men momentarily.

Reuben fell at Jesus' feet, burying his head in the dirt beneath him. For some reason he didn't need anyone to tell him which of the men was Jesus – his heart told him. And before this Man he felt more unclean than he ever felt in his life. But courage rose for the briefest of moments and he dared to speak, ignoring the furore that was developing around him.

"Lord, if you are willing you can make me clean."

Then it happened. Jesus leant towards the ground – and touched the deformed, diseased and dirty leper.

No one had touched Reuben in years – not a handshake – no kiss of greeting – no friendly clap on the back – no contract agreed by the slapping of a sandal in the palm of his hand. No human contact of any kind – only in his memory. And nowhere in his memory had he ever felt such a touch!

"I am willing; be clean."

Five simple words – only five; yet the most beautiful words Reuben had ever heard – and spoken with such unrivalled compassion that Reuben thought his heart would break with their tenderness. The rivulets of tears coursing down his dirty cheeks didn't stop him looking into the eyes of God; and Reuben knew he would never be the same again.

In the seconds it took to hear those life-changing words and feel the touch of the Son of God, Reuben knew he was a leper no more!

Rising from the ground, he saw toes on his feet; unblemished skin on his hands; and he could feel his nose rise in his face again. And the stench of death had disappeared. Able to stand straight once more, with strength and vigour filling his frame, Reuben's cries of delight and praise reached the corners of the market place.

Trying to quieten him, Jesus spoke again, telling Reuben

not to tell anyone, but rather to go to the priest to have his healing confirmed. Jesus knew there would be sceptics, so keeping to the Mosaic law was essential if Reuben was to re-enter normal life again.

He headed for the priest's home, shouting, dancing, laughing – yes, he was actually laughing; he didn't think he could remember how – but laugh he did! The priest heard him coming before he reached his house and couldn't believe what he saw. It was Reuben. But it couldn't be! The last time he had asked Josh about his brother he was told that Reuben was so full of leprosy now that they didn't expect him to survive the coming winter.

Yet here he was – clean, or so it seemed.

Hurrying outside the city, as the Law required, the priest carefully examined him and confirmed what Reuben already knew – he was no longer a leper. The next eight days were like eight years, as Reuben completed the rituals required for cleansing; but once the sacrifice had been offered for his atonement before the Lord, it was time to go home.

Reuben stood in disbelief at the door of his little house. He had never allowed himself the luxury of imagining that this day could ever come. Stepping inside, he was like a man reborn – health renewed; hope restored – and all because of Jesus.

AD 2008

The Swiss theologian Emil Brunner once said: "What oxygen is to the lungs, such is hope for the meaning of life."

To have hope removed is to lose an absolute essential, and without it we merely function rather than live. For some, hopelessness is the result of circumstances that cannot be changed, whether because of a diagnosis of illness, or a crisis within the family or at work.

However, millions across the world face a hopelessness brought about by man's continued inhumanity to man. Their control is not lost by circumstance, but by the design of others. Can hope ever be restored for them?

Ladli tiptoed anxiously towards the door of her home. She knew it was important not to interrupt her husband during his daily puja, but the factory whistle had already blown and he appeared not to have heard it. Workers at the pipe factory were two a penny. If Bir was late he could lose his job, and they would lose their home. She coughed loudly, trying to divert him from his ritual prayers to the Hindu god, Lord Ram. His folded hands and bowed head were evidence of his longing to find union with god, and perhaps a way of escape from his miserable daily fight to survive another day.

"Come, come, Bir… come! The whistle has blown. We are late!"

The sound of his father-in-law calling him pulled Bir away from the broken cork board that served as his family shrine. Bowing repeatedly as he backed out through the makeshift door, Bir grabbed the little battered cup from his wife's hands and quickly gulped down the lukewarm water that she offered him. Yet again another day's hard work would start on an empty stomach.

Her father smiled towards her as Bir ran on ahead of him towards the factory gate. She glanced tenderly at him, silently recognizing that the old twisted man before her was actually only fifty-eight. Twenty-five years of working twelve hours a day making concrete pipes had taken its toll on this kind man, whose only wish in life was to make things better for his family. With a wave of the hand he headed after Bir, coughing for all he was worth – the concrete dust having done its worst on his lungs.

Ladli relaxed once more and leaned against the rim of the concrete pipe that was her home, as the sun started to dispel the shadows that cloaked her village.

"If only the darkness in my life could disappear as easily as the night does," she whispered under her breath.

Depressing thoughts were coming more frequently with every day that passed. Everything seemed hopeless. The pretty young Indian woman knew that her life was already mapped out for her, and nothing or no one could change it.

She was Dalit.

As she stood looking into the distance, all she could see was large sections of concrete pipes. Some of them were bricked up at one end, with rickety doors made of rusted corrugated tin or old planks of wood at the entrance. A feeble attempt at privacy, but at least it kept out the wind and rain. Pipe after pipe, stretching into the distance, each one a family home, each one a prison. And there was no escape, nor even hope of parole.

Glancing beyond the concrete, the great city of Hyderabad lay eleven miles south of where she stood – yet she knew she would never walk its streets. Oh, maybe if she was brave enough, she might walk its backstreets! But if found in the wrong place at the wrong time, she knew her life would be in danger. Sometimes she thought of running away – but to what? Her life's course was already determined. Nothing would ever change that.

She was Dalit.

Even her own father told her to stop dreaming as she was growing up. The gods had birthed them as "untouchables". They were not even clean enough to be included in the caste system. Lower than the low; lower than the animals; only fit to deal with dirt, and therefore to make all those they came in contact with impure.

"Maybe if we work hard enough, we will do better in the next life," he used to tell her.

"Why did he ever bring us to this awful place?" she whispered to herself. "Surely the village beside the city dump wasn't as bad as here?"

Ladli was too little to remember the days before the pipe village, when her father scavenged on the city's dump. It was her mother who told her of the day the man came to the dump and announced to the men present that he could change their lives. He promised to give them enough cash for a dowry to help their daughters marry well; a job to pay back the loan, and a home for their families. To a man with two daughters it was like a dream come true! So, for the past twenty-five years, her dear father had been working in the concrete pipe factory to pay back his loan, with barely enough rupees left to feed his family.

His oldest daughter had been married off to a butcher, and he was glad when Bir's father had agreed to take Ladli as a wife for his son with so little dowry. Ladli understood why her father had told her to accept her lot in life – because dreams don't come true. He had proved it.

Sighing deeply, she pushed back what served as a door and went inside. Thankfully, she wasn't very tall and could nearly stand up straight if she kept to the middle section of the pipe. In a short time her eyes grew accustomed to the dark as she made her way past the cork shrine to the sleeping quarters. The little bundle resting tight against the brickwork started to move and Ladli leant down to stroke it.

"Hello, Mama," said the gentle voice of a young child.

"Hello, Aboli, my little flower," Ladli replied as her daughter pushed back the rags that served as her bedding. "It's time to get up, sleepyhead. We need to walk to the water pipe, and who knows, we may find something to eat on the way."

The little girl had the most beautiful eyes, like melting chocolate, and her smile made Ladli's frown lines disappear. Aboli was the bright little spark in Ladli's miserable existence, and the only dreams she dared to dream were really for her. How she wished that she could allow her child to dream dreams; how she wished she could see a different future for her – one where she wouldn't be despised and looked down on by others. A future where she could live in a proper home and have food every day. Perhaps even a future where she could go to school. But there's no chance of that happening – because… Aboli was Dalit.

"OK, Aboli, enough of my silly daydreaming. We must fetch some water to wash your pretty face, and to cook some rice for Father's dinner when he returns tonight."

The child smiled at her mother without understanding what she was talking about. *What's daydreaming?* she wondered, as she picked up her little jug from beside the door.

Ladli's pot balanced safely on her head as she made her way back from the standpipe at the other side of the village. Aboli tried to mimic her mother, but still needed to steady the pot with one hand to stop it from falling on the ground and spilling its precious cargo. The task took a lot of concentration, but she was pleased with the progress she was making. Soon she might be able to balance a larger jug, if they had one. Then, in a momentary lapse, Aboli stumbled, just managing to catch her jug before it landed on the ground.

"Aboli! Be careful!" her mother shouted, not wanting to have to make a second trip back for water.

"I'm sorry, Mother, I thought I heard singing – and the jug just slipped."

"It must be those Christians back again," Ladli said, with distinct disdain in her voice. "Just keep walking."

Aboli looked longingly at her mother, pleading with her to stop. "But, Mother, the singing is so pretty, and they have some bread. Please let us stop, just for a little while – I'm hungry."

In the end it was the child's big brown eyes that did it. Ladli gave in and headed toward the muted sound of singing.

"Don't tell your father we stopped here; you know he wouldn't like it. Christians are devils, he says!"

"But they seem kind, mother. They always help us."

"That may be – but don't tell him."

The piece of warm naan bread tasted good, as Ladli nibbled on it nervously. She was grateful that today Aboli's tummy would not rumble until Bir returned from work in the evening, when they would have their daily meal of rice. Sometimes there would be something to mix with it, but often not. Aboli was right, Ladli thought, as she watched her daughter play with some of the other children. The Christians were always friendly and kind, but her husband would be displeased if she stayed to listen to their "god talk", so she lifted her water pot onto her head once more.

"Aboli," she called. "Aboli, we must go now; come quickly!"

The look on her mother's face told Aboli it was pointless to argue, and the child meekly rose from the dust, lifting her little jug as she did so.

A few minutes later, Aboli's face screwed up as the cold cloth wiped across her face, around the back of her neck and was finally wiggled in her ears.

"Take off your clothes, little one, and I will wash them."

"Ah, Mama, do I have to?" replied the disgruntled child, realizing she would have to sit inside the hot pipe while her clothes dried in the sun.

"Aboli, we may be poor, but we don't need to be dirty," replied her devoted mother, wishing at that moment for even one change of clothes for her pretty little girl.

As Ladli worked at removing stains from a T-shirt that had once upon a time been worn by some child from across the world who probably had dozens more, she heard the singing yet again. The music was soothing and happy, settling her somewhere deep inside her being. Wondering what they had to be happy about, she strained to listen to the words of the song.

The name of someone called "Jesus" was repeated a number of times. She assumed that he must be one of their gods, but no – the song says he is God's only son. *How could that be? There are hundreds of gods, and they have hundreds of children – some even born at the temples.*

The T-shirt twisted easily in her hands as she forced the water from it.

"Bir's right," she murmured aloud, "these people are mad," but she couldn't help but listen on as she hung Aboli's clothes up to dry.

"The God who created the heavens and the earth is the same God who made each one of us – and he loves every man, woman, boy and girl," came the words, floating through the air.

Ladli was stunned by the words. Never before had she heard such a thing. God didn't love her. He couldn't even know that she existed. She was Dalit.

"In God's book – the Bible – we read that: 'God loved the world so much that he sent his one and only Son. If we believe in him, we shall not perish, but have eternal life.'"

By now, Ladli was trembling. What she was hearing couldn't be true. It was so confusing. Dalits didn't go to Nirvana; eternal life was for the gods and maybe the Brahmins, not for her. It wasn't possible.

She was Dalit. Unclean. Impure. Dirty. Less than the animals. Without hope for today and all the days ahead of her.

Hadn't her own father told her so?

"Yes!" the preacher shouted, "God loves you – even if you are Dalit."

Ladli covered her mouth to stop the scream that wanted to escape, shocked at what the voice had just said; afraid that her very thoughts were visible to this "Christian devil".

"Mama, can I come out yet?"

Aboli's cries startled Ladli back to reality. Glad to be distracted from the words that were shaking her inside and out, she quickly disappeared inside the pipe, away from the noise and the foreign thoughts that were trying to get her attention.

But it wasn't that easy. She couldn't leave them behind. They haunted her awake and asleep. She was even afraid that Bir might hear them echoing inside her head, as she lay beside him.

God loves you. God loves you. God loves you.

The next day, Ladli and Aboli took the long way round to the standpipe to fetch water. All Aboli's pleadings were in vain, when she heard the singing again. Instead, the child was frightened. Her mother appeared angry, harsh; pulling her back towards home and quickly inside. But hiding away didn't stop the words hounding her.

God loves you. God loves you – even if you're Dalit.

A week had passed since Ladli first heard those fateful words, and try as she might, she couldn't avoid hearing the singing and even more phrases from what the man called God's word – the Bible. As she was getting Aboli dressed one morning, there was a loud knock on what passed for her front door.

"Good morning, Ladli," came the friendly greeting that

met her as she glanced outside.

The pastor – for that is what they called their "holy men", she discovered – and with him two women stood smiling a few feet from the entrance to her home. Ladli's heart beat faster, fear rising in her throat. *What could they want from me?* she thought. Before she had time to reply, the kindly gentleman was speaking again.

"We wanted to talk to you about a special programme that is to start for women in the village," he said.

"Oh, but I am not Christian," Ladli stammered, feeling foolish that her nervousness was showing. "It wouldn't suit me."

"You don't need to be Christian to join," replied one of the ladies. "It's for all women who want to learn new skills to help their families. We will teach you how to sew and how to grow vege…"

"But I don't have any money," Ladli interrupted.

"You don't need to have money," the other lady interjected, "it's all quite free. We have sponsors."

Ladli didn't know what a sponsor was, and couldn't believe that anyone would be prepared to teach her anything… and it was free… and she didn't have to be one of them to join. It must be a trick.

"My husband isn't here," she said, "you'll have to speak to him."

With that she quickly shut the door, before they could say any more.

All day, Ladli fussed about her home, afraid to go out in case she met any of those Christians. She had no idea why she felt so uneasy. They had only ever shown her kindness. Perhaps that was the problem; no one had ever shown her kindness before.

She was Dalit. And she didn't know how to respond; it was all so alien to her.

Hearing the factory whistle blow, Ladli poured a little rice into the water boiling in the battered tin bucket she used for cooking. Smoke and steam filled the pipe, eventually finding little escape routes between the bricks that blocked the back of the pipe. How she wished she had some vegetables or ground curry leaf to making the meal more appealing. The words of the lady from earlier rolled around in her head.

"We will teach you how to grow vegetables!"

Ladli shook herself, trying to make the words disappear. Hearing the first of the men returning from work, anxiety overwhelmed her once more. *What if the pastor and the women come back to speak to Bir? He will be so angry. He told me not to have anything to do with the Christians.*

Her head was spinning as Bir's hand pushed open the door.

Conversation was not Bir's strong point. He went to work in the factory for twelve hours every day; ate his rice on his return; rehearsed his evening prayers; and dozed on and off, before getting ready for bed. Occasionally he threw a ball with Aboli: the ball he had made for her birthday by winding strands of dry, coarse grass together. It didn't bounce, but it was fine for a game of catch.

For Bir, every day was the same; there was little to talk about. So on this particular evening he didn't notice his wife's lack of conversation as he ate his rice.

Suddenly a knock came at the door. Bir jumped in shock, while Ladli dropped her plate, making a clanging noise as it hit the concrete floor. Visitors were uncommon in this place of poverty and hopelessness.

The remnants of the smoke from the cooking fire rushed over the visitors as Bir opened the door. Standing in front of him was a smartly dressed man, accompanied by a woman.

"Good evening," he said, bowing his head in greeting to Bir. "I am Pastor Thomas, and this is my wife. Ladli invited us to speak with you about allowing her to attend the project for women in the village."

Standing behind Bir, Ladli stifled a gasp. Before she could explain herself, the pastor was quickly telling Bir all about the project. He was speed-speaking, before the door could be slammed in his face.

"The project," he explained, "is to introduce skills to women that would help them care for their families, boost the family income and provide the money to allow their children to go to school."

School! Ladli's ears opened wider. She hadn't heard that before. Aboli could go to school! Learn to read and write! Maybe one day get a real job. Not a Dalit job, but a real job.

The next thing Ladli was aware of was Bir shouting at the pastor, calling him horrible names and telling him that they didn't need the Christians' charity. The rickety wooden door fell to pieces as Bir tried to slam it in their faces.

And Ladli realized that her nervousness and dizzy head was all because, for the first time in years, she was allowing something to form in her heart – hope. Hope that maybe things could be different. But as the door fell into pieces, so did her dreams… once again.

Bir moved away from the rest of the men as they drank hot tea over their lunchtime break. He was tired of hearing about the women's project. As far as he was concerned, those who allowed their wives to go to this "Christian" thing were traitors to the Hindu way of life.

"So you would rather stay poor, Bir. You want your child to stay all her life in this village? What if you can't afford the dowry for her wedding, what will you do then? Will you give her to the temple and let the gods look after her?"

The words of Bir's friend stung him deeply. There was no doubt about it, Lord Ram had not answered any of Bir's prayers for himself or Aboli.

He was still Dalit. No hope in this life, and precious little in the next. How he longed to be able to give Aboli more and to see Ladli smile. It had been a long time since he had seen her smile. If Ladli wanted to go to the women's project, then he wouldn't stand in her way. The whistle blew, and he headed for home.

Three months had passed since the night Bir had come home from work and announced that Ladli could join the women's project. Now, her fingers were calloused from needle pricks, but Ladli had never been happier. She held tightly to the little bundle as she rushed home to make Bir's dinner, excited at the prospect of what she had to show her husband.

"Hide, Aboli... he's coming!"

The child giggled in the darkness at the end of the pipe as her father bent low to enter his home. Before his eyes became accustomed to the darkness, she could wait no longer.

"Surprise!" she shouted, jumping out on her unsuspecting father.

"Child, what are you doing?"

"Do you like it, Papa? Do you? Do you?"

Bir couldn't stop the mist from forming over his eyes as he looked at his precious child dressed in a simple blue and white checked dress.

"It's my school uniform, Papa. Mama made it! Isn't it beautiful, Papa, isn't it?"

Choking on his words, Bir pulled the child close in a gentle embrace, his tears falling onto her black shiny hair. "Yes, Aboli, it's beautiful."

Lying awake in the darkness beside her husband, Ladli allowed her thoughts to linger over the changes that had been taking place in her life. She was learning to deal with new emotions: happiness... contentment... even excitement! But with all of that, she knew there was still something missing; something she could never have, because of the man lying beside her. She could not have Jesus in her heart. Bir would never allow it.

As she drifted into a deep sleep, she repeated the words Pastor Thomas had given to her earlier in the day. They were words of Jesus: "I have come to give you life. Life in all its fullness."

"That's what I want," she whispered under her breath, "the life that Jesus gives."

Ladli didn't hear Bir coming in from work on that particular evening. She was singing – something she normally only did when Bir wasn't at home. She loved to sing about Jesus. As she was stirring the rice pot, she was singing at the top of her voice.

"Stop that, woman! Do you hear me? I won't have you mention that name in this house!"

Ladli felt herself being lifted from her knees by her hair, as her husband's rage boiled over furiously. Fear gripped her as Bir tried to push her out of the door. Her toes caught on the pipe rim as she was hurled across the floor in anger, twisting her back as she landed on the ground outside.

Pain seared through her body. She couldn't move.

Weeping silently in the dust, she could hear Bir scold Aboli, telling her what an evil mother she had for singing about Jesus beside the holy picture of Lord Ram. As time went by, Ladli heard Aboli's crying stop, and she prayed to God for the first time.

"Protect my little flower, Lord."

She lay on in the dust, unable to move. And the rain fell, mingling with her tears. Darkness had fallen and the dust had turned to mud, before Ladli heard the door of her home open.

"Get up, woman!" Bir shouted. "Don't make a fool of me. Come inside!"

Ladli tried courageously to move, the pain shooting

through her body causing her to cry out against her will. She was afraid to speak. She had never seen Bir so angry before.

"Get up, I said!"

"I can't," she replied, her words barely audible.

Bir cursed as he caught hold of Ladli's arms and dragged her inside, ignoring her squeals as her back was bumped over the rim of the pipe.

Lying just behind the door where her husband had dropped her, Ladli shivered. She couldn't feel her legs, yet great surges of pain coursed through the rest of her body. Soon, the sound of Bir's snoring echoed through the pipe, while the gentle breathing of Aboli brought her comfort. God had answered her prayer and protected Aboli from her father's angry rage.

"Please help me, God," Ladli prayed.

A sense of someone's presence filled the place, and Ladli was no longer afraid.

Next morning, Ladli heard Bir repeat his daily prayers to the cork shrine, while ignoring his injured wife, still lying where he had left her the night before. He was not normally an unkind man, but Ladli felt that she had pushed him too far with her Christian songs. Her pain was her fault – or so she tried to convince herself.

She kept quiet until he left, and then she tried once more to push her body into the sitting position – but to no avail. She still couldn't move, and a sense of helplessness overwhelmed her, until she could no longer contain her sobs.

"Mama, Mama! What's wrong?"

As Ladli turned, she saw Aboli standing over her, terror filling her eyes. The child was remembering her mother's cries from the night before, playing out the violent scene in her mind. Ladli painfully lifted her arm to stroke the child's cheek.

"Don't worry, little one. I'll be OK. I just need to rest. You get dressed and then bring me a little drink of water."

Aboli didn't move. Instead, she sat beside her mother, whimpering like a sad little puppy, stroking her mother's head with her small warm hand. The gentle comfort lulled Ladli into a fitful sleep.

Bir felt ashamed. As he worked, it was more than the weight of his labour that etched the strain on his face. Ladli was badly hurt, and it was completely his fault. She was a good wife. She had never given him trouble before. And he had frightened Aboli as well. Eaten up by guilt, he worked like a man possessed. Yet pride had stopped him from attempting to put things right. He hadn't even checked to see if she was OK before he had left for work. *But*, he argued, trying to justify his actions, *he couldn't tolerate her being a Christian – it was wrong. Surely she could see that?*

Aboli was startled by the knock at the door.

"Ladli," the voice cried, "Ladli, are you in there?"

Aboli recognized the voice and went to open the door. Seeing her mother's friend from the sewing class, she fell into her arms weeping.

"Quickly! Quickly!" the child cried, "Mama's hurt."

Ladli's friend cradled her head gently, trying to find out what was wrong with Ladli. Piecing the story together, she realized that Ladli needed help. But there was no doctor in the village and no money to pay for one, either.

"Aboli, stay with your mother. I am going to get help."

In a flash, the woman was gone, and Aboli felt the fear grip her once more. She started to cry. What if the lady didn't come back? What would become of them? Ladli was trying her best to comfort the distraught child when they heard voices approach.

"Pastor Thomas… you came!"

The sight of the pastor bending down low to enter her home brought to the surface all the emotion that Ladli had been trying to hide from her little girl, and her tears flowed like rivers. Stretched out on the floor and filthy from lying in the mud the previous night, Ladli felt more unclean than ever before. Yet standing over her was a man whose look of compassion was hitherto unrivalled in her life.

"Ladli, I need to bring you to the church to pray for you. Will you let me lift you, please?"

"No, Pastor, no! I am filthy… unclean… unworthy. Pastor – I am Dalit."

"If God loves you, child, then so do I," explained the humble, gentle man.

Ladli felt him slip his arms under her bony frame and tried not to squeal as the pain surged through her once more. Her dirty, wet clothes stained his pristine white shirt as he lifted her so carefully. For a brief moment she felt so ashamed of her condition – both inside and out – but then something amazing happened. As Pastor Thomas struggled out of the pipe, Ladli felt the most overwhelming sensation of God's love for her.

Ladli, I have loved you with an everlasting love; you are precious in my sight.

"God knows my name," she murmured. And looking at those who had stooped low to help her – an untouchable – she saw that God does more than talk.

The next few hours were the most difficult and yet the most wonderful that Ladli had ever experienced. In the tiny wooden structure they called "church", prayer was continually made for Ladli's healing. She couldn't go to hospital and there was no doctor. Only God could help her now. The women gently washed her, carefully combing back her long hair from her face. They gave her a little water to drink, and she managed to smile as Aboli tucked into some breakfast.

Between the times of prayer, Pastor Thomas read more from God's book. One verse in particular grabbed Ladli's attention.

"Those who come to me I will never turn away."

Ladli reached up and caught hold of the pastor's arm.

"Does that mean me, Pastor?" she asked, as a single tear escaped from the corner of her eye.

"Of course it means you, Ladli."

And he kept on reading, but Ladli didn't hear him, because she was too busy coming to God. And she knew she had not been turned away, because her whole being was filled with a peace that she had never experienced before. She was no longer afraid – not even of Bir, because nothing he could ever do to her could take her saviour from her. Not now, not ever. And she felt clean.

"Mama, Mama! It's time to wake up."

Ladli stirred, unsure of how long she had been asleep, and for a moment thought she had perhaps dreamt the whole thing. But it wasn't a dream. She was still lying on the mat at the church – and her heart was still full of peace.

But something was different.

Her legs – she could feel them! And the pain – it had almost gone! Still groggy from her sleep, she struggled to sit up, pushing her arms against the floor. Confusion turned to delight as two of the women helped her to her feet. She felt weak – but she could stand.

It can't be true, she thought, *God has healed me.*

Prayer turned to praise in an instant as they realized what had happened. God, the God of the miraculous, had answered their requests for Ladli's healing. She was now new, inside and out. Their songs of thanksgiving echoed through the village.

Bir's chin was virtually attached to his chest as he made his way home after work. His feet dragged in the dust, slowing his pace. He was afraid to go home; afraid of what he might find, after leaving Ladli in such a state earlier that morning. All kinds of thoughts tormented him, and a sick feeling in his stomach had plagued him all day. As he neared his front door, he was surprised to see the customary smoke seeping through the cracks. Pulling the rope handle, he gasped, stepping backwards, almost afraid to enter.

There in front of him was Ladli, on her knees stirring the pot. She looked radiant and was wearing the most beautiful red sari. It wasn't possible! She had been so ill when he left this morning; but before he had time to speak, Aboli jumped up to greet him.

"Papa, the most wonderful thing happened!"

The child spoke at great speed, explaining all that had happened that day. Her big brown eyes as wide as clocks, she related the story of the miracle: of how one minute her mother couldn't walk, and how the next she was standing on her feet.

Bir was dumbfounded. He was seeing and hearing things he had known nothing of, previously. He had no idea how to respond. His head was spinning with confusion and disbelief, and yet here she was – his wife – looking better than he had seen her in years.

"Where did you get the sari?" was all he could think of saying.

"One of the ladies from the church gave it to me. Mine was all dirty," Ladli replied, waiting for her husband to fly into a rage, especially at what she was about to tell him.

"Bir," she said quietly, "I am sorry I made you angry, but I need you to know that I have asked Jesus to come and live in my heart. I am a Christian now."

Turning to take her cooking bucket from the small fire, Ladli waited. But Bir remained silent, alone with his thoughts, for what seemed like a long time.

"What's wrong, woman? Do Christians not feed their husbands? Do I have to starve in my own home?"

Ladli served Bir his rice, with a silent prayer of thanks and a smile. He did not return it, but in time she believed that he would.

The young charity workers could never have been prepared for what they saw, the day they visited the pipe village north of Hyderabad. They were stunned into silence as they realized that families actually lived in these discarded 12 x 5 sections of sewer piping, over the wall from the factory that held many of them in bonded labour. The sights and smells of living on the bottom rung of humanity assaulted all their senses and left them reeling.

It made it difficult for them to concentrate on all the skinny pastor was saying, as he described the women's empowerment project, and the difference an education would make for Dalit children.

Singing came from one of the pipe homes – beautiful singing. They were invited inside by a pretty lady in a red sari, with a beautiful daughter who had big brown eyes. It was hard to keep the nausea at bay, as their eyes grew accustomed to the dark and their bodies to the stifling heat and smell of hot concrete.

A little gauze bag holding three small oranges hung from a nail close to a battered old tin bucket, the lady's only cooking implement. Beside the ashes of yesterday's fire lay half a melon covered in smoky soot. Yet the woman kept smiling and singing, a light coming from her eyes that was inexplicable in the darkness of her physical circumstances.

"What was she singing about?" one of the visitors asked

the pastor after they had left. "What has she got to be so happy about?"

"Why, Jesus, of course," he replied, a wide smile crossing his face. "Ladli no longer lives a hopeless existence. She has hope for her future and for that of her daughter. She knows she is loved and accepted by the God who made her. "She is no longer Dalit; no longer untouchable and unclean!"

And it's all because of Jesus.

About "Hopeless"

C. AD 31

Read for yourself the story of the man with leprosy as it is recorded in Luke's Gospel, chapter 5:12–15.

Other related biblical references:

The Old Testament law concerning leprosy – Leviticus 13–14

The Shema – Deuteronomy 6:4–9

AD 2008

I am deeply grateful to Sarah Orr, manager of the Wesley Owen bookshop in Coleraine, Northern Ireland, for sharing with me the true and moving story of Ladli, from the pipe village north of Hyderabad. The plight of the Dalit people of India is heart-rending, yet the gospel of Jesus Christ is changing the lives of many people who live in such hopeless circumstances.

Important biblical references in Ladli's story:

John 3:16, John 10:11, Jeremiah 31:3, John 6:37.

Worthless

C. 995 BC

"Be afraid, Goliath! Be very afraid. I am David – and today I will chop off your head!"

The little boy's forced, gruff voice bounced off the walls, echoing down the long corridor, as his playmate ducked beneath the pebble that whizzed past his head. They both gasped in horror as a marble urn crashed off its stand, smashing into pieces on the stone floor. Before they had a chance to escape, the large frame of the boy's nanny appeared from nowhere, blocking the passageway.

"Mephibosheth! What are you up to, boy? Haven't I told you not to play with slings in the palace?"

"Run, Phibi!" his friend shouted, turning on his heels and leaving him to face the music alone.

Mephibosheth knew it was pointless to run. Nanny Phoebe mightn't be able to catch him now, but he couldn't hide for ever – and his rumbling tummy told him it was tea time. It was a simple matter of priorities.

Remembering that Nanny's bark was always worse than her bite, he decided to put Plan B into action. Dropping the sling behind his back and looking up at her with big soulful eyes, he knew it was time to use the charm offensive: running towards her, throwing his small, skinny arms around her neck, giving her a tight squeeze.

"I'm sorry, Nanny, I forgot," he said, planting a kiss on her rosy cheek, "and… Dan told me to do it! I promise I won't do it again."

"Promise?" the older woman asked, totally taken in by his sweet innocence.

"I promise," he replied, breathing a sigh of relief. "But don't you think that my sling shot is getting better, Nanny? It's nearly as good as David, the son of Jesse's."

Suddenly, the chubby woman took the young boy by the forearms, giving him a shake that frightened him, instantly bringing tears to his eyes.

"Don't ever mention that name again, Mephibosheth! Your grandfather doesn't allow that name to be used in this house – you hear?"

"But David is Daddy's friend, Nanny."

"That's as maybe," she stammered, "but he's no friend of King Saul, and your father would be wise to take note of it. So, speak no more of him! Come now, Cook has barley bread and goat's cheese waiting in the nursery for tea."

The little boy wiped his nose on his linen tunic and put his small hand into that of the woman, who was more of a mother to him than a mere palace employee. Sighing as they walked towards the nursery that was housed in the north tower of the palace, Mephibosheth couldn't help but wonder why his grandfather disliked his father's friend so much. After all, David was a hero! He had killed the giant Goliath and saved all of Israel. And just before he left to battle once more with the

Philistines in the Valley of Jezreel, his father had hugged him and whispered in his ear.

"Don't ever be afraid of David, Mephibosheth," he said. "He is my true friend; he will never harm you."

The barley bread tasted dry in his mouth, as he looked longingly out of the tower window over the rolling hills into the distance. Somewhere out there his brave father was fighting the enemies of Israel, in the name of the Lord Jehovah. Soon he would return and tell him stories of the victory. But for now the little five-year-old missed him.

Raised voices in the corridor brought Mephibosheth back from his quiet thoughts, giving rise to a sudden sense that something was wrong. Getting up from the table, he went to open the door. Nanny Phoebe rushed in, almost knocking him over. She was flustered, her cheeks red, and breathing noisily and fast.

"What's happening, Nanny?" Mephibosheth asked, pulling at her skirts. "Is there news of Daddy? Is the battle won?"

Kneeling down to hug the child, she tried to find the words to calm him.

"Don't fret, child. You know that King Saul and Prince Jonathan are the bravest soldiers in the land. Let's get you to bed – all that fighting with Goliath has you tired out!"

As Phoebe tucked her precious charge under the blankets, she struggled hard to stop the frowns finding their way back to her warm, round face. The news from Jezreel was bad – no, it was dreadful. The Israelite army was taking heavy losses. Their warriors were no match for the Philistine chariots, and many were falling at the hands of expert archers. Bodies littered the

Valley of Jezreel, and to make matters worse, the courier was reporting that many of their own soldiers were deserting. King Saul and his three sons had retreated with their defeated army to Mount Gilboa to make a last stand.

As her chin trembled, the royal nanny moved away from Mephibosheth's bed to silently weep for those three young men, whom she had once cared for, too. It seemed just like yesterday that they were boys.

Was only Ish-botheth to be left of Saul's dynasty? she wondered.

There was little sleep in the palace at Gibeah that night.

Mephibosheth woke while darkness still surrounded his room; the oil lamps had burnt out, but the sun remained asleep. Sitting upright and rubbing his still-groggy eyes, the boy could hear shouting and wailing and the sound of horses' hooves clip-clopping around in the courtyard below. He was afraid.

Nanny burst into the room, making him jump and scooping him up into her arms.

"Mephibosheth, we have to take a journey – we must leave here quickly! It's not safe to stay!"

As they headed towards the stairs, Mephibosheth saw servants running in all directions, shouting, crying, carrying hastily filled bags as they ran. He couldn't understand what was going on, and he responded in the only way that made any sense.

"I want my daddy!" he cried, tears streaming down his face.

"I'm sorry little one, but we must leave – the Philistines are coming. We must get you to safety."

Phoebe was still running, puffing and panting as she went, the boy seeming to grow heavier with every step she took. His struggling and crying added to the ordeal for the aging nanny. How she loved the child! Yet she had no idea where she would take him, or how she could keep this heir to the throne safe, now that his father was dead. Yes, Jonathan was dead! Saul was dead – and no doubt his only remaining son, Ish-botheth, wouldn't last long either.

Empty thrones turned men into murderers! Nanny couldn't let them get their hands on Mephibosheth. They needed to put distance between themselves and the palace.

Ignoring the boy's crying, she made her way along the corridor to the east tower. The gardener, little Dan's father, was hitching his hay cart to a donkey.

"It'll draw less attention than a royal wagon," he had said to her when the sad news arrived from Gilboa, and she was sure he was right. No one would ever think of looking for the heir to the throne in a hay wagon!

"Hurry, Phibi, hurry!" shouted Dan, his voice piercing through the noise that was going on around him.

Hearing his friend's voice, Mephibosheth lifted his head off his nanny's shoulder for a second to look for Dan. Nanny was hot and sweaty, puffing and panting as she ran.

The stone flooring was rough and uneven where it met the outer door. In the briefest moment of time, Mephibosheth felt Nanny jolt forward, as the toe of her sandal caught on a loose stone. Her arms opened wide to break her fall – but it was too late! Mephibosheth dropped through the air, crashing to the ground, Nanny barely able to stop herself from falling on top of him!

The searing pain took his breath away, shock holding back his tears for a moment. By now Nanny too was squealing in pain – pain for Mephibosheth, pain for Saul and Jonathan, and for the unknown future that lay ahead of them.

But only Nanny, Dan and his father stopped to care for the injured heir.

He couldn't move. His feet were dangling, twisted at the end of his bare legs. And the pain – he couldn't stand the pain. Nausea rose in his throat. His head was spinning – and the enveloping darkness took him away from the pain.

By the time Mephibosheth tried to force his eyelids open, the sun was up. His head ached; his back was twisted against a pile of hay; his feet felt how the urn had looked the day before – smashed and in pieces. He was afraid to move. The ends of his legs seemed to be on fire: the searing pain seemed ready to plunge him into darkness once more.

Then he felt something bump underneath him, as his mind started to process what had happened. He had fallen… they were running away… Dan was calling his name.

"Dan," he mumbled softly, "Dan, where's my daddy?"

Instantly his playmate was by his side, his face etched by frown lines usually owned only by adults.

"Phibi, oh, Phibi, I thought you were dead!" the child cried, wiping big tears away with the back of his grubby hand.

"But daddy said it's just your legs that are hurt – you'll be OK, Phibi, you'll be OK."

"I hurt, Dan – I want my daddy."

Before he realized what was coming out of his mouth, the young boy replied: "But Phibi, your daddy is dead – and the king too. The Philistines won, Phibi – they beat us!"

The gardener pulled the donkey over to the side of the dirt track, as the screams of the young child filled the air. This time, they knew it wasn't just the pain of his injury that was causing the heart-wrenching cries – it was the sound of his young heart breaking.

Mephibosheth forced a smile, as he watched Dan swing the sling above his head. The pebble flew across the field, just missing the target by inches. Dan groaned, kicking the dust.

"Ah, Phibi, I'm just not as good a shot as you. C'mon, give it a go!"

His little crippled friend silently shook his head, while Nanny Phoebe looked on with a sadness that had rarely left her face since that night three months ago in Gibeah. She was grateful that Machir, a kind distant relative of Mephibosheth's mother, had taken them in, granting them food and shelter. But as she looked around at the barren landscape, she felt they were living in a God-forsaken place. Lo Debar – it was well named, she thought, for there was "no pasture" here, only dust and gravel. They seemed to eat the stuff morning, noon and night – it got into everything! Gone were the rolling, lush grasses of Gibeah, with the sound of sheep bleating around the palace walls. Only goats could survive here, in the hilly, coarse scrubland and forests beyond.

At least they were safe. Some fifty miles and more from Jerusalem, with the Jordan River and the unwelcoming terrain of Gilead between them and danger, Phoebe recognized that they would finish their days in obscurity.

Anyway, the word is bound to have got out about Mephibosheth's fall – a crippled heir is no threat to anyone.

But what really worried her was whether she would ever see a smile on the child's face again. With time, he would learn to get around somehow – on crutches, or cart, or donkey. But he had lost so much more than his mobility. He had lost his home, his father, his future – and his sense of worth.

Mephibosheth was safe, but that was all. And so the months disappeared into years and boyhood merged into manhood for the son of Jonathan, in the barren desolation of Lo Debar.

The sound of the men celebrating tore at Mephibosheth's heart. Turning towards the wall, he pulled his cloak over his head to shut out the noise of their singing. Their victory party was well-deserved, for they had aided King David in his fight against the marauding Moabites to the east, bringing peace to their corner of Israel. Mephibosheth's problem was that he had to stay behind as usual, with the women, children and old men. How tired he was of hearing, "You can't do that, Mephibosheth – you're just not able."

Can't – can't – can't! How he hated those haunting words.

Long gone were boyhood dreams of fighting in battle beside his brave father; of ridding his country of violent enemies; of governing his land in a time of peace. In their place were nightmares: of a forgotten prince, a useless body and a worthless life.

Not that he had an axe to grind with the man on the throne. It appeared that King David was every bit as good a man as his father had once told him. He hadn't come to the throne by acts of treachery, as some had tried to do; rather, by patiently waiting until the time was right. And in these past nine years Israel was at last entering a time of peace and prosperity. To the west, Philistia had fallen; to the east, Moab had been defeated; to the south, Syrian-dominated Edom had been subdued; and to the north, Zobah had been put in its place. The kingdom of Israel had been established, united and strong.

But Mephibosheth, the crippled grandson of King Saul, had no part in it.

Sitting at the city gate one day, Mephibosheth was listening to some of the men negotiate business deals, haggling and arguing around the price of their transactions, when he noticed horses approaching. With the dust billowing around them, he couldn't make out who they were; just that they were in a hurry.

Business stopped momentarily, as the men conducting it rose in greeting, grateful also to escape the dust cloud created by the approach of the visitors.

"Ziba, is that you?" questioned a town elder, as he moved towards the white-haired man who was dismounting. "I haven't seen you since I visited the palace in Gibeah. How many years ago is that?"

"Too many years, old friend. And, yes, it's me – you do me an honour by recognizing me after all this time."

Mephibosheth's ears pricked up at the mention of Gibeah. Introductions were in full swing, as the other more important members of the gathering were introduced to Ziba and his companions. By the time it was Mephibosheth's turn, he had pulled himself up onto his crutches and was already aware that the man who was receiving all the attention had once worked for his grandfather at the palace.

Only this time he hadn't come from Gibeah, but from Jerusalem, on the King's business.

"You must be Mephibosheth," he said, moving forward to greet the young man. "You were a small boy the last time I saw you. I bring you greetings from the King."

Shocked by this unexpected greeting, Mephibosheth stepped back, almost tripping over his crutches, only to be saved from an embarrassing fall by Dan's father.

The evening couldn't come quickly enough for Mephibosheth. Ziba had been invited to wash and rest in Machir's home while supper was prepared. Indeed, if the king himself had been in Lo Debar that night, the banquet could not have been more splendid. Machir, known for his hospitality, had exceeded himself on this occasion, with foodstuffs of every description available to his guests. But Mephibosheth barely touched a morsel.

How could King David know about him? Why had Ziba come? Was he to be arrested? Would his miserable existence soon be over?

In those hours Mephibosheth's mind became a tangled mess of unanswered questions that he was too afraid to ask, while Ziba seemed more interested in boosting his own importance by filling the ears of those gathered with news of all the happenings in Jerusalem.

"So, Mephibosheth," Ziba finally remarked, turning to face him at last, "You are the reason I am here. King David wants to meet you!"

For the next hour Ziba explained how the king had sent for him one day, asking if there were any of Saul's family still alive. He was nonchalant as he finished the wine Machir was serving; almost as if it were an everyday occurrence to be summoned by the king. Mephibosheth, however, had broken out in a cold sweat.

Continuing, Ziba explained that the king seemed interested in showing God's kindness to any family that remained of his friend Jonathan. He thought it was something to do with a promise he had made years ago.

"That's why, Mephibosheth, I told King David that you were alive and living in Lo Debar. But don't worry, my boy; I made sure he knew you were a cripple!"

The patronizing sting of Ziba's final remark made Mephibosheth's stomach churn; the pride of being Jonathan's son dissolved by one word – cripple!

Sitting once again in a borrowed cart, Mephibosheth watched as Lo Debar disappeared into the distance. Through many years, that dust bowl had become his home and place of protection; it was also where he was now leaving his young son, Micha. And he had no assurance that he would ever see him again, despite Ziba's promises to the contrary. He was, after all, the remnant of a previous royal dynasty, and his grandfather, King Saul, had sought to end David's life on more than one occasion. Was this merely a trick to give David payback time?

But an inner voice plucked from a childhood memory told him not to be afraid. It was the voice of his father – and for the next few miles it brought him comfort.

Crossing the Jordan at Beth-shean, Mephibosheth remembered the days when this part of the Transjordan Valley was dangerous territory, having been captured for a time by the Philistines. In the distance, Mount Gilboa rose majestically above the Valley of Jezreel; it was the first time he had seen the place of his father's death. The sun shone high above him, but clouds covered his heart as sorrow was rekindled.

They journeyed on, through rolling countryside dotted with small villages and towns where they stopped to rest and eat. Mephibosheth knew he was slowing Ziba and the others down, but for once he didn't really care. He was in no rush to get to Jerusalem, and the journey was giving him time to see parts of Israel that he had not seen since he was a boy. By the time they reached the hills around Gibeah, Mephibosheth knew that he was in home territory. He was surprised at just how much he recognized from his boyhood. He gasped as they passed Saul's palace; his old family home with its four corner towers, no longer looking impenetrable. How sad it was to see the grand old place now falling into ruin, with weeds and rubble denying its history as the palace of the first king of Israel.

Fun… laughter… love… security… family! All only memories now.

Jerusalem lay eight miles south of Gibeah. King David chose the neutral land bordering both the northern tribe of Benjamin and the southern tribe of Judah to be his capital city and seat of government. Mephibosheth chuckled at the wisdom of the king. Moving from Hebron and capturing the city from the Jebusites was a diplomatic move, uniting the kingdom. It appeared that David was not out to make enemies – especially of his own kinsmen.

But could Mephibosheth be sure that he thought the same way of old foes? He would soon find out.

Mephibosheth barely noticed the grandeur of the building, as Ziba led him through the corridors towards the throne room. Sweat was dripping from his brow as he tried to keep up. He was convinced that the palace guards could hear his heart pounding in his chest as they walked beside him. Anxiety was making him dizzy; fear was making him drool. Sitting so long in the cart had unsteadied him; his crutches didn't seem to be working in co-operation. He felt such a mess; certainly not fit to be presented to the king.

What was he doing here? Why had he agreed to come?

Panic and terror seized him, as the huge cedar doors opened before him. Afraid to look into the face of the king, Mephibosheth threw himself prostrate on the stone floor before the throne, his crutches flying out to either side, his body numbed to the pain of the fall; awaiting his fate.

"Is it you, Mephibosheth?" came a gentle voice from above him.

"It is, my Lord; I am your servant!" he replied, his lips so tight against the cold floor that he wondered if his trembling words could be heard, his face contorted with fear.

"Don't be afraid, Mephibosheth," the voice said again, as he felt helping hands raise him from the ground before the king.

Daring to risk the swiftest of glances throne-ward, Mephibosheth was shocked to see that the face of the man, who must be the king, had a warm smile and thoughtful eyes.

"Don't be afraid; I've brought you here to show you the kindness of God because of Jonathan, your father. I want to return to you all the land that was your grandfather's. But you, yourself..."

"Oh, here it comes," he groaned, "what has he in store for me?"

"You shall stay here at the palace with me and eat at my table – as one of my sons."

With his head bowed to his knees before such grace, Mephibosheth was overcome: "But, Lord, who am I, that you should treat me so? I am worthless – of no more value than a dead dog!"

But the king would not listen to his protests. Instead, he sent for Ziba, and in the presence of Mephibosheth he told the man who had described him as a mere cripple that he and his sons would be Mephibosheth's servants for life. They were to care for his property and work his fields, that his family might be provided for.

Ziba was to be a servant again, while Mephibosheth – the cripple – was to sit at the table of the king. Always! Mephibosheth knew that what the king was offering was more than a free lunch! To sit at his table, as one of his sons, meant not merely protection, provision, and a secure future – it meant acceptance. David wasn't taking on Mephibosheth as part of his family because of what he could or couldn't do, but rather because of who he was – the son of his dear friend Jonathan. And there before the throne, he witnessed grace and mercy bound together with fulfilled promises.

Later that day, Mephibosheth clunked his way to the great hall. He had on his back clothes fit for a prince; he walked along cedar-lined corridors draped with purple-dyed cloth; was welcomed at the table set with gold; enjoyed the company of the king's sons, in the presence of the "man after God's own heart". Not once had anyone mentioned the words "cripple" or "can't"!

And now, sitting at the table, he bowed his head once more, not in shame, but in thankfulness; overwhelmed by his present position and his future hope. He had been summoned from the desolation of Lo Debar by the king; made worthy by another, accepted because of grace, and loved in spite of himself. In mercy, Mephibosheth was now a child of the king

No longer worthless!

AD 1980

Having delivered over forty babies, and given birth myself, it's hardly surprising to hear that when a baby is born the mother's first question, after finding out the gender, is: "Is he (or she) all right?" The standard reply is usually, "He (or she) is just perfect," causing a communal sigh of relief in the labour ward that all has gone well.

I think it's true to say that we live in a world that is obsessed with perfection – or at least its own notion of perfection. There seem to be unwritten rules about what is regarded as acceptable, suitable, or even perfect. Scattered around us are invisible moulds that we should be able to fit into if we are to be seen as having worth or value in our society.

There's the mould of "good" parentage – but if you miss that one, then perhaps you might be able to squeeze into the "good" education one, which could spring you into the "good" job mould. You're almost there, now, as from here you might make it to the "good" marriage mould. Throw in the nice house in a "good" location, and your perfect little world is starting to build around you. A further asset is fitting into the financially secure mould; that way, you won't be a burden to society. In fact, it will set you up for a happy life – or so we are told. Once all of this is in place, you just need to squeeze yourself into the final mould to complete your dream – the perfect children mould. They in turn will quickly learn to look out for their own little acceptability moulds.

But what if you've missed the "good" parentage mould and never managed to get those needed GCSEs for the "good" education leading to the "great" job mould; meaning that the house, location and perfect partner never seemed to come along? How do you feel then? Or what if your children don't fit that "perfect" mould? What will our perfection-obsessed society say about that?

Maybe some of us have heard their reaction already; words thoughtlessly tossed in our direction, now indelibly stamped on your lives: "You are worthless… good for nothing… no use to anyone." What do we do then?

"What are you going to do with her?" the young consultant asked, with a tone of condescending pity in his voice, as he faced me over his large desk.

"I'm sorry?" I replied. "I don't understand your question."

"Well, you're not going to keep her, Catherine, are you?"

I couldn't believe my ears. If he had been talking about a sick puppy, or an ailing pet, I might have understood his question. But this was my baby daughter he was talking about!

"Do you have children, Doctor?"

"You know I do, Catherine, but that is not relevant to this conversation."

"Are you going to keep them, Doctor?"

"Now you are being silly. You've got to realize that *this* child will ruin your life! Her problems are huge. You really should give it some thought."

By this time, my blood was boiling. Anger, hurt and disappointment were pushing me to the edge of rage; I was trying desperately to maintain some dignity and not cry in front of this man. But all my efforts at composure failed as the hot tears brimmed over.

"Just what do you want me to do with her, Doctor? Put her in a box and post her somewhere?"

The chair crashed to the ground as I pushed it backwards in an effort to get to my feet, baby in arms. The sudden noise and movement startled Cheryl, making her cry, while loud, shaking sobs came from somewhere deep inside me. I tried to place her against my shoulder, while grabbing the parked buggy at the same time. The extra pair of hands that were needed to open the door came from the doctor, who had suddenly realized that his "expert" piece of advice was not what a heartbroken young mother needed to hear.

"Please don't leave in such a state – you are taking what I said all wrong – I didn't mean…"

"You didn't mean what, Doctor? That my child is somehow inferior to yours and doesn't deserve the love and care of her parents? Just give her away – and that will solve the problem!"

He eventually reneged, opening the door. As he did so, I launched my final shot in fury: "Don't send me another appointment. I never want to see you again!"

Navigating the busy outpatient department with a buggy in one hand and a distraught child in the other was disastrous. It seemed as if every pair of eyes was fixed on me, and I don't blame them. We must have looked a sight: sobbing mother, crying child and a buggy with a mind of its own, rolling all over the place, threatening to trip up anyone who came close.

When I eventually found a reasonably quiet place to stop

and strap Cheryl into the delinquent buggy, I looked at our beautiful, blue-eyed blonde daughter with the same love as any first-time mother. A few months earlier, we had been told that she was "handicapped and would never be normal"; shock and sorrow may have been our initial response, but there was one thing that dreadful diagnosis did not change – our love for her. And therefore there was no way that I could accept what I had just heard.

Cheryl was not some kind of worthless bunch of mixed up genes – she was our daughter! And every day God gave her on this earth, we would continue to love and care for her.

They say "a change is as good as a rest", and as I packed I knew that being on the staff at a Christian holiday centre catering for around two hundred people each week would definitely be more change than rest. But I was looking forward to the experience. It had been a hard five months since Cheryl's diagnosis. Our lives, dreams and plans had all been thrown into turmoil, and as time passed we were beginning to see just how disabled our lovely child was becoming. Maybe things would look brighter in a different place, surrounded by different people.

The drive from Stranraer and on down through England was long and tiring, but our hearts lifted when we turned into the long, leafy driveway of the private boys' boarding school that was to be our home for the next three weeks. It was easy to imagine the rich and famous driving up this magnificent tree-lined road leading to the castle-like building at its conclusion. The setting was jaw-droppingly beautiful. The "oohs" and "aahs" continued as we were led into the Great Hall for a welcoming cup of tea and the first staff meeting, before the guests arrived. Touring the private indoor swimming pool and fabulous sports facilities made one feel a little jealous that such accommodation was available to only a small group of children in our society. It didn't seem quite fair – until, that is, we were shown our sleeping quarters! The previous squeals of delight turned into gasps of dismay. The dormitories were nothing short of tawdry! Hard wooden bunks, squashed into small spaces, surrounded by defaced hardwood lockers. I doubt if any of Her Majesty's Prisons were as barren as these living quarters. Suddenly, jealousy turned to pity at the thought of some normally privileged ten- or eleven-year-old being left here for months at a time, without the love and care of family.

At that minute, I determined that we would spend as little of our three weeks as possible in this part of the school!

My husband spent his day busy with all kinds of everything, while I looked after Cheryl. Whenever possible, I helped in the kitchen, chopping, scraping, peeling the enormous amounts of food that were consumed each day by holidaying teenagers. The young people on staff loved Cheryl, and she dutifully smiled for them at the appropriate times, causing ripples of laughter, encouraging the circle of responses to continue. So, by the end of the week, the young people rose to the occasion by giving Cheryl a surprise first birthday party! There was a cake with one big candle, and a very large teddy bear, and the singing of "Happy Birthday" brought the watched-for smile from her little round face. I was touched by their thoughtfulness, and yet, unknown to the party-goers, this birthday marked a significant milestone in an unsure future.

"If she doesn't sit up by her first birthday, then there is a big question mark over her future physical development," the doctor had told us a few months earlier.

Not only could Cheryl not sit up unaided, she couldn't even hold her own head up. At the party my well-practised smile hid an extremely heavy heart.

The middle week of the holiday centre was a family week, and I was encouraged by the prospect of seeing others of my own age along with young children, instead of only teenagers. The place was buzzing with excitement as folk started to arrive on the Saturday. I noticed that there was a large group attending from a Nigerian church in London – with lots of babies! It wasn't long before they had organized a crèche out on the lawn during the morning Bible readings.

"Catherine, we don't need you this morning," the cook said. "Why don't you join the other mums on the lawn? It's such a beautiful day, and you'll enjoy the company."

I didn't need her to ask twice, as I was really looking forward to taking Cheryl to meet the other babies and toddlers – and of course to having some sensible chat about teething and the like – the kind of stuff teenagers know nothing about. So, with Cheryl's frilly sunhat in place and the sun-brolly attached to her buggy, we both headed out into the garden.

I was really quite excited. The sun was high in the sky on this beautiful August day, and I chatted to Cheryl as we walked towards the happy group playing on rugs spread out on the short grass. As I neared the group, one rather large lady in colourful Nigerian dress came towards me. I smiled as we met, only to hear her tutting in response. I was rather surprised, unsure of what the problem was, but she spoke before I had time to offer a greeting.

"Shame, shame," she said, shaking her head vigorously. Looking straight at Cheryl she continued: "Children like that shouldn't be born… 'tain't right… 'tain't right, I say."

Standing behind the buggy, I held on tightly for all I was worth, dumbfounded at what I was hearing – my mouth lying wide open, unable to say a word as she continued: "Better if she'd died at birth, don't you think?"

Aghast, I barely managed a stammering reply: "No! I don't think!"

Never before had I made such a quick about-turn, running back up the path that led to the dormitory building. The verbal assault on our little one dealt yet another vicious blow to my already fragile emotions. *"Better if she'd died at birth"* was competing with *"this child will ruin your life"*, as other insensitive, thoughtless comments crowded my mind. How could people think like that about a helpless child?

Hadn't she enough to put up with, without people judging her life as worthless… her existence pointless?

As I lifted her floppy little body into my arms and held her close, I was eternally grateful that she could never be hurt by another's words, because she was oblivious to their meaning. In that instant I refused to believe that Cheryl was some freak of nature, or even some kind of divine mistake.

"Surely they're wrong, Lord?" I questioned, as the old dorm

bed creaked under my weight. "Lord, show me that Cheryl's life is not worthless."

An unusual strength filled me as I lifted the Bible onto my knee, looking at it over Cheryl's small form. While not normally agreeing with the ad hoc approach of throwing your Bible open and hoping a verse jumps out and hits you between the eyes, I did just that. I wasn't surprised when the pages fell open at the book of Psalms, as I'd derived comfort from them frequently in recent months – and these were the words that I read in Psalm 139:

> *For you created my inmost being; you knit me together*
> *in my mother's womb.*
> *I will praise you, because I am fearfully and*
> *wonderfully made;*
> *Your works are wonderful, I know that full well.*
> *My frame was not hidden from you, when I was made*
> *in the secret place,*
> *When I was woven together in the depths of the earth,*
> *Your eyes saw my unformed body.*
> *All the days ordained for me were written in your*
> *book before one of them came to be.*

"Listen to this, Cheryl!" I exclaimed, making the poor child jump as I raised my voice in excitement. "You're no mistake, Sweetheart. God knew exactly what he was doing when he made you – it says so right here in Psalm 139. It says right here that God formed you; he knew your little frame before I did, when it was just a bunch of cells – it wasn't hidden from him. You were no surprise to him. And you know what, Cheryl? God knows exactly how many days you will have. You were meant to live, and not to die. That lady was wrong, very wrong!"

I doubt she understood a word I was saying, but the excitement in my voice caused a whopper of a smile to cross her face. And I laughed and laughed, as I danced around that drab old room, knowing without a shadow of a doubt that the child in my arms was no worthless reject. She was a daughter of the King – a special creation – an object of his love. One day, he would call her to feast at his table – for always!

About "Worthless"

c. 995 BC

Read the story of Mephibosheth for yourself, as told in 2 Samuel 4:4 and 9:1–13.

AD 1980

Cheryl is our eldest daughter. The full personal story of the Campbell family is told in my first book, *Under the Rainbow*.

Helpless

C. AD 32

Reumah thought she heard voices.

The early morning sun attempted to creep under the door curtain, as she stretched away the sleep of the receding night. Pushing herself upright, she strained to listen to the whispering coming from the courtyard, just a few feet away.

"Listen to me, my son; no one would blame you if you asked the rabbi about a bill of divorce. This has been going on for too long now – she will never bear you children!"

Reumah caught her breath as the words pierced her heart. Frozen to the spot, she listened on in sheer horror.

"Leave it, Mother," replied the voice she recognized as her husband's. "Reumah is my wife – can't you see that? I love her. She'll be well again… some day."

"Love, love! What has love got to do with it, Dan? It's been six years now – six years! And you haven't been able to touch her in six years!"

The whispers had become louder, and Reumah was distraught as she listened to Dan defending her to his mother. She was broken-hearted. Knowing that she was a useless wife to this strong, young fisherman, she felt totally helpless to do anything about her situation. Rising to her feet, she staggered, pulling back the curtain to face her accuser.

"Please," she cried, "please tell me what I can do to change things. You have no idea how much I want to be a good wife to your son – but I don't know what to do!"

Shocked that Reumah had heard the altercation between him and his mother, Dan reached forward to comfort his young wife. In an instant, his mother caught his hand before it could touch Reumah's shoulder.

"Don't be foolish, Dan. You'll be unclean!"

Reumah knew the woman was right and pulled back, as Dan tried to ignore his mother's harsh advice.

"I'm sorry, Dan – I can't risk being the cause of making you ceremonially unclean – it's too high a price. Perhaps your mother is right; you…"

"No, Reumah; when I married you I promised to care for and keep you in the manner of the men of Israel. I will not abandon you!"

"Then we must pray that the Lord Jehovah will show us mercy," she replied, her voice shaking.

Drawing the door curtain, she watched her dear husband turn and walk away from her once more. Falling onto the straw-filled mat that occupied virtually the total floor space of her small bedchamber, Reumah covered her head in her hands, weeping uncontrollably. She tried to stifle the sound of the sobbing, but it was pointless… the house echoed with the noise of despair.

Sitting at breakfast, Dan could only push the food his mother had made for him around his plate. Neither of them spoke, each filled with their own personal pain from the helplessness of the situation.

In an effort to compose herself, Reumah reached for the small bowl of water and little brush, to try to remove the stain from her bedding – the stain that betrayed the cause of all her heartache.

A short time later, Reumah tied a small pile of clothing into a bundle and quietly crept out of the house. Avoiding the main street that ran directly down through Capernaum to the Sea of Galilee, the weary young woman took a roundabout way through the narrow backstreets towards the water. It made the journey twice as long, but at least she didn't have to suffer the indignity of men standing aside while she passed them on the street, afraid that she might touch them. It seemed that everyone in her home town knew of her personal, private problem – that she was in the virtually permanent state of niddah.

Reumah understood only too well that the Mosaic law rendered a woman ceremonially unclean for a whole seven days during the normal female period of menstruation. It was meant to be a time apart; to rest from normal household duties, and also from physical intimacy of any kind with her husband. For any man to sit where she sat or to lie in her bed or even touch her during the niddah would mean that he too would be unclean. Such behaviour would bar him from entering the synagogue or approaching God in any way until he had completed the rituals required for his cleansing. It was just a normal part of life for a Jewish woman; no big deal, really, *if* her body was functioning as nature intended.

As Reumah passed the customs station on the edge of the town, she winced at the teasing remarks of a few Roman soldiers trying to entice her to join them for "some fun"! Keeping her head down, she quickened her pace. How ironic that the men of her own race avoided her like the plague, yet these foreigners would have her in their beds in a minute! Her face flushed with embarrassment, while her heart longed for the attention of only one man – her beloved Dan.

The previous day's storm had cleared the air, leaving freshness in its wake, and the sun sparkled on the water like jewels as Reumah approached the edge of the lake. But the pleasantness of her surroundings did little to relieve her burden, while the unpleasant conversation earlier on continued to trouble her greatly.

If I were Dan's mother I would probably feel the same way, she thought, as she tiptoed over the smooth stones lining the water's edge. The previous six years flashed through her mind, reminding her of the week her problem had started. She was disappointed that her niddah had arrived, secretly hoping that perhaps during that particular month she would have been able to announce that she was pregnant. She loved Dan so and knew that he would make a great father. But instead, the pain and bleeding continued… on… and on. And not only was Dan still without a son – he barely had a wife, either!

Flopping onto a large stone, Reumah was pulled from her thoughts by the sound of children. She smiled as she watched her friend's son Joel toss pebbles into the water, clapping his hands in glee as they splashed a short distance from him. His mother and a few other ladies waved a greeting at Reumah, who always sat far enough away from them to prevent complaint. Hers was a lonely existence.

Setting her outer mantle beside her on the rocks, Reumah

shortened her tunic a little by pulling it out over her belt and set about washing her clothes in the fresh water of the Sea of Galilee. This far north, the water was still really Jordan water, as it entered the lake not far from where she was sitting. Some distance offshore, she could see a fishing boat anchored and the men working at bringing in a catch. Lately, Dan had taken to fishing at night. He said it was to have a better chance at landing barbels, good for selling beyond Capernaum, but Reumah wondered if he just wanted to avoid being in the same house as her at night. Spreading her garments on the rocks to dry in the hot sun, her mind returned to those three dreadful words: "bill of divorce"!

Covering her head with her mantle once more, she sat planning – planning what more she could do to find a cure.

Memories of foul-tasting tonics made by her mother-in-law made her empty stomach churn! She had already tried every recipe suggested by the older women of the town – and suffered the results of them for days afterwards! She remembered with horror how the skin on her abdomen had peeled with the astringents she had applied, causing as much pain on the exterior as the cramping did on the interior! Yet she knew she must try again, or she might lose her darling husband and be relegated to this miserable existence for ever.

Later that day, she plucked up the courage to ask her mother-in-law to visit the priest for her yet again.

"Please, ask him to list all the cures the Talmud suggests," Reumah begged. "I must try again, for Dan's sake."

Hearing her son's name mentioned, the older woman softened and complied with her daughter-in-law's request, heading off for Rabbi Joel's house. The old man of the synagogue was bound to know of some of the more unusual "cures" for Reumah's condition. For the first time in years, both of the women in Dan's life had lightness in their spirits as they determined together to find a solution to what had become a difficult family problem.

"You can't be serious, Reumah! An ostrich egg?"

"Dan, please try! Rabbi Joel says that if I carry the ashes of an ostrich egg in a linen cloth over the summer then my bleeding will stop."

"Where am I going to get an ostrich egg?"

"Perhaps some of the merchants travelling from Egypt through to Syria would be able to get one for us."

"How much will that cost, Reumah?"

"I don't know, Dan – but then perhaps you don't think I'm worth it!"

"You know that's not true, Reumah. But last month, Rabbi Joel had you eating dishes of Persian onions boiled in red wine, and you were sick for a week!"

"Please, Dan; I'll work hard at weaving more of the cloth those merchants like, and maybe we can trade it for an ostrich egg."

"You're already working your fingers to the bone, Reumah, and it's only the foreigners that will touch your cloth! I'm worried about you."

"Don't be, Dan. I'd do anything to be well again – to be your wife again!"

Dan breathed a frustrated sigh, looking longingly across the courtyard at his wife, whose form seemed to grow frailer by the day. His annoyance stretched to his mother, who was encouraging all these foolish attempts at a cure, each one more far-fetched than the last. Yet secretly he hoped that one of these ludicrous suggestions would give him back his wife.

Now where on earth was he going to get an ostrich egg?

Years had passed since Reumah had removed the linen bag containing the ashes of the ostrich egg from around her waist and thrown them in the fire in disappointment and disgust. Her patient husband had worked hard to provide extra finance for all the "cures" she had tried, again and again. He had even gone against the wishes of his own father when Reumah asked if she could see a doctor.

"Don't you know what the rabbis say about physicians, Dan?" his aging father shouted across the deck of the boat, as they fished together one night. "The best of them is only fit for Gehenna! Do you hear me, Dan – only fit for the place of the dead!"

Dan said nothing, every muscle in his tired body groaning under the weight of the catch, as they pulled the net on board.

"You might as well give your hard-earned money to those fish as to waste it on doctors!" the old man continued.

Yet Dan knew he could not give up. So everything they had went on paying for Reumah to see doctors.

Because of attitudes like those of Dan's father, there were very few Jewish doctors. Instead, Reumah had to face the indignity of seeing the doctor who accompanied the Roman garrison. He was male and Gentile, but she knew that every doctor had taken an oath, following the teaching of Hippocrates, not to take advantage of women. So, in fear and trepidation she went, month after month, first to the Roman doctor in Capernaum, and then to various Greek doctors, wherever she could find them. Each of them had a different idea of what the problem was, and with every new doctor Reumah would become hopeful that maybe… just maybe… she would be cured this time.

She was the model patient. Everything they asked of her she did – whatever the personal consequences to her health. Often the treatment was more severe than the illness and, rather than getting better, she was growing worse. And now all their money had run out. She had even sold her last piece of jewellery: the beautiful gold necklace that her father had given to her at her wedding. She was sure that he would have understood. But even that was to no avail – the niddah continued, and she felt utterly helpless!

Now bent over, looking more than twice her age, with her skin pale and her weakened limbs barely able to carry her, she set off for the tedious two-hour walk to Tabgha for the final chance of a "cure". As she made her faltering way out of the village she stumbled, losing her balance. A child came running to her aid, and as she looked up from the ground her eyes filled with emotion. The girl was around twelve years old; beautiful and elegant. Her long dark hair was plaited behind her finely sculptured face, and she smiled in kindness as she helped Reumah steady herself. *Such a lovely child*, Reumah thought as she thanked the girl. *I'm sure her father is proud of her*. Suddenly a man's voice called out from the steps of the synagogue, interrupting her thoughts, and the girl ran off in response. As Reumah looked in their direction, she recognized the man. It was Jairus – the ruler of the synagogue.

"You have a beautiful daughter, sir. May God bless her for her kindness."

"Thank you! I'm sure he will."

Reumah continued along the rough path leading to the neighbouring village, thinking of all that the past twelve years had given her. Jairus had been given a beautiful blessing in his daughter, while she had been given the dreadful curse of her illness. Yet she wasn't bitter – just intensely sad.

Reumah was starting to regret setting out on this journey, when she reached a clearing that swept all the way down to the lake. It was a natural amphitheatre, sometimes used for entertainment or speech-making. So she wasn't really surprised when she saw a bit of a crowd gathered there – well, it was quite a big crowd, really. Sitting to rest for a while, she found herself captivated by the rabbi standing not too far from the lake's edge. It had been so long since she had heard a rabbi teaching, as she wasn't allowed to enter the synagogue or attend the festivals because of her "uncleanness".

But this man was like no other she had listened to before. And his face – even from so far back on the hill, she could see that he had something about him… she just couldn't put it into words. Rising to continue her journey, Reumah decided that she would ask Dan about this strange new rabbi when she returned home.

For now, she had a "cure" – a final "cure" to seek.

The fact that she was unable to walk at speed meant that Reumah arrived in Tabgha at the hottest time of the day. It was a small village and so, in no time at all, she found what she was looking for, but as she knelt in the dirt of a stable, Reumah started to weep.

"Oh Papa, I'm glad that you can't see me now – kneeling here among the dung of a white she-ass! Why did you name me Reumah? I'm far from 'exalted' here among this filth – to bear the name 'humiliated' would have been better for such a one as I!"

The despairing sound of her weeping travelled beyond the rickety lean-to of the stable. She had reached the end of herself, and this was definitely the last straw. For twelve years she had put off the foul, humiliating task of searching for a complete ear of barley corn in the dung of a white she-ass, but as her hands and clothes absorbed the stench, the reality sank in. She had not felt like a wife for many years, and now she felt less than human. Success was far from sweet as she wrapped two filthy ears of barley corn in a little cloth and set off for home. How she was going to swallow them, she had no idea!

"What's the smell, Mother?" Dan asked as he arrived home from mending his nets.

"Your wife," she said, with an unusual amount of sympathy in her voice. "I'm burning her clothes, and she's trying to wash the smell off her skin."

"She didn't, did she?"

"She did – she found a farmer with a white she-ass – and walked to Tabgha to retrieve her 'cure'."

"Tabgha! How did she manage to walk all that way?"

Concern was etched in lines across Dan's face, but his conversation was interrupted by his father racing into the house.

"Did you hear about Zebedee's sons?" he panted.

"No, Father, I didn't – mother and I are talking about..."

"Never mind what you were talking about. Listen! Zebedee's boys have left home to follow some rabbi from Nazareth! Imagine – they've given up fishing to go after a carpenter's son!"

Dan's father was very distressed at what he had heard about his old friend's sons. There was no doubt that it would be catastrophic for his fishing business. His agitation turned Dan's attention from Reumah's ordeal that day to the local goings-on in Capernaum.

"And they aren't the only ones! Big Peter and his brother Andrew are giving up fishing as well! Did you ever hear the like of it? They've all gone mad! This 'Jesus', or whatever his name is, apparently told them that he would turn them into 'fishers of men'! Nonsense! I never heard such nonsense before!"

Dan's mother appeared with a little cup of wine in an attempt to calm her husband down. She had never seen him so agitated before. As everyone started talking at once, Reumah wakened from her state of exhausted sleep. Drawing back the curtain, she sat on her little three-legged stool to listen to all the commotion.

"I heard him preach at the lakeside while I was mending my nets," Dan interjected. "He seemed sound enough; talked a whole lot of sense, Father."

"Sense! What sense is there in taking a man's sons away from their father's business?" the old man spluttered, wine spraying all before him.

"Some of the women at the market said that he performs miracles," added Dan's mother, as she scraped away at some fish she was preparing for tea.

"Don't listen to such talk – magic tricks aren't miracles, woman!"

Miracles! The word made Reumah sit up bolt upright!

"What miracles, Mother?" she asked, her question alerting them to the fact that Reumah had joined in their discussion.

"Well – there was that servant of the centurion – you know, the one from the garrison here; it seems that Jesus just said the word and when the Roman got back to barracks, the man was back on his feet! And then some sabbaths ago the men returned from the synagogue to find Peter's mother-in-law sick with a fever and..."

"Leave it, woman, don't fill the child's head full of nonsense – hasn't she been through enough, without hearing all this?"

"Please, Mother, tell me – what happened to Peter's mother-in-law?" Reumah pleaded, rising to her feet in anticipation.

Ignoring her husband's brusque comment, Dan's mother turned to Reumah: "Jesus rebuked the fever – and she got up and served them dinner!"

Reumah caught hold of the doorpost, swooning in shock. "Why has no one told me of this man before?"

"I thought you knew, Reumah," Dan replied, his voice soft with emotion. "Everyone's talking about it – crowds of strangers arriving in the town every day."

"And how am I meant to know about crowds? I never leave this place!"

Tears stung her eyes at the thought that people were being healed right here in Capernaum, and she had known nothing about it. "Is Jesus the man I heard preaching by the lakeside today, when I was on my way to Tabgha? Was that him, Dan? Have I missed him?"

Dan felt ashamed that he hadn't told her about the carpenter-cum-rabbi from Nazareth, but he was genuinely afraid of building up her hopes only to see them dashed once more. His father was right; she had been through enough; but before he had time to reply, the old man spoke again.

"And how can you approach this rabbi? Even if he could help you, you are ceremonially unclean! He can have nothing to do with you!"

With the harshness of his words, Reumah felt the room spin and her knees give beneath her, as she melted into floods of tears. And for the first time in years she felt arms around her, as her mother-in-law wrapped her up in love and pity.

Reumah couldn't sleep. The slop-bucket beside her bed held the evidence of the "success" of the full ear of barley corn retrieved from the white she-ass! She felt so ill – and utterly dejected. There was only one thing left for her to do. She *had* to see the rabbi from Nazareth. Her mother had once told her that the tassels hanging from the outer mantle of a holy man's clothing had special powers to heal. According to her mother-in-law, Jesus had already shown such power, so she determined that, for the first time in twelve years, she would risk the crowds, unclean or not!

"If I can just touch the edge of his garment, I will be healed," she whispered, as sleep overwhelmed her emaciated, exhausted body. Every day seemed like a year, as Reumah waited for Jesus' return to Capernaum.

"He's preaching all over the country, Reumah," Dan told her, trying to encourage patience in his wife. "I've been asking around; no one seems to know when he is coming back, but he *will* return, Reumah, because folk say he's made Peter's house his base."

Then, late one afternoon, Dan's mother rushed into the courtyard, so breathless she could hardly speak. "Reumah!" she cried. "Reumah, he's here! Jesus has returned – he's down by the lake! Go quickly, girl, but be careful; the place is crowded!"

Jumping suddenly to her feet, Reumah became dizzy and stopped momentarily to steady herself. Fear, excitement and emotion caused her heart to beat faster and her palms to sweat. Could this be her day? Was it really possible that she could be made well after such a long time?

Making her way down the main street to the lake, Reumah didn't care whom she met. Covering her face with her mantle, she tried not to catch anyone's eye, in case they recognized her as the women who was "unclean" and prevented her from getting to Jesus. It wasn't long before she reached the edge of the large gathering of people frantically attempting to get closer to where the voice was coming from.

That voice… there was something about that voice!

A few people scowled as she pushed past, but her heart sank as Jesus came into view. Looking at him, she knew it would be impossible to touch his garment! He was sitting in a boat, just offshore! With her heart in her boots, she listened to what the teacher was saying. It was something about a farmer going out to sow seed, but she wasn't quite sure what it meant, as disappointment clouded her understanding. And out of the corner of her eye she saw Dan on one of the other small boats that had gathered around Jesus.

Despair forced her weak body down onto a boulder as she watched the men with Jesus lift anchor and set sail for the far side of the lake. She had no idea how long she had been sitting, when wind and rain began to beat on her frail body. Rising to make her way home, she saw the boat tossing to and fro in the distance as the storm beat against it. It was difficult to keep her feet on the path towards town. She padded her way along the walls of houses to prevent the fierce wind lifting her off the ground. Then suddenly, like the crack of a whip, the storm stopped – dead! Surprised, she looked up, to see the clouds speedily rolling back in the sky towards the mountains. Behind her the moon shone brightly on a still sea, while the last of the rain rolled off her chin. Reumah had never experienced anything like it – she had no idea what had just happened.

But the man on the boat did!

Reumah found it hard to sleep. She was more and more convinced that Jesus held the answer to her future. She just had to get near enough to touch him – just once. She knew that was all it would take – just one touch! Desperation fired her resolve, but also expanded her feeling of helplessness. She simply had to get to Jesus!

Lingering in the side streets, Reumah watched as more and more people arrived in Capernaum. She saw the sick and the lame sitting in the streets, the air electric with expectation. Hope was etched on faces; smiles carved where heartache had previously languished. Children sang songs and played in and out between the legs of their mothers. Reumah looked on longingly. Perhaps one day she too could know the joy that these women took so much for granted… perhaps?

Suddenly a wave of excitement passed through the waiting crowd.

"He's back!" they cried. "Jesus has returned!"

"It's now or never," Reumah whispered into the shawl which covered her face.

The narrow streets of Capernaum almost groaned under the weight of such crowds, as people surged forward to see Jesus. Reumah didn't even notice the skin of her arms scraping along the black basalt walls as she squeezed her way towards Jesus. Rooftops creaked as people vied for a high position, just to catch a glimpse of this man from Nazareth.

Then, just as she thought she was close enough, a man stepped right in front of Jesus – and fell at his feet! She recognized him – it was Jairus, the synagogue ruler, whose little girl had helped her the day that she had stumbled on her way to Tabgha.

He looked distraught! Reumah could only hear snippets of his conversation with Jesus – something about his daughter – dying! Pain struck Reumah's heart. That beautiful, kind little girl, dying? Surely not!

Continuing to move forward, she heard Jairus ask Jesus to

come to his house: "Come and lay hands on her, that she may be healed, and she will live," he pleaded.

Panic set in! It had taken her so long to get this far, Reumah didn't want Jesus to head off in another direction. She didn't want to hold Jesus back from going to Jairus' house – she just needed to touch his clothes – that was all! By this time others were pushing and shoving, and she was starting to be carried backwards by the moving crowd! With all the strength she could muster, Reumah stretched her hand forward and touched the tassel on the fringe of Jesus' mantle with her bony fingers!

And it happened! In an instant! *Immediately* she knew! She had been healed! A strange feeling of heat and energy passed through her body. The heavy, dragging pain that had been her companion for twelve years was gone! The telltale trickle of niddah had dried up! Strength entered her bones, her back straightened and the lines of helplessness were erased from her face! The moment she had been waiting for most of her adult life had come in just that – a moment!

She wanted to shout out and tell everybody, but instead she turned to quietly retreat – and as she did so, the slightest hint of fear entered her heart. Would anyone believe her? She had been sick for so long, and everyone knew that her case was "incurable". But just as she tried to push back from the crowd, she heard that wonderful voice call out.

"Who touched my clothes?"

Frozen to the spot, Reumah stifled a gasp with her hand.

Surely, he couldn't have known – my fingers barely reached his garment, she reasoned in her panic. And remembering what her father-in-law had said a few days earlier, she started to shake.

She, a ceremonially unclean woman, had touched a rabbi!

Her thoughts were interrupted by the commotion that was now playing out before her. Jesus' disciples responded, virtually accusing him of foolishness. They argued with him over how the street was crowded in the extreme – people bumping into Jesus all over the place, while Jairus was still on his knees, troubled by the delay.

But Jesus knew that power had gone out of him and persisted in looking for the one who had touched him. And Reumah had the sneaking suspicion that Jesus already knew it was she, as his eyes met hers in the crowd. Moving forward to own up, Reumah trembled visibly with fear. Now it was her turn to be on her knees before the only one who could heal – the one who had changed her life. And she simply told Jesus all about it.

She told him about her sickness; her helplessness; her attempts at cures; and how, when she had heard about him, she knew, finally, that she only had to touch the edge of his garment and she would be healed. And as she spoke to him, the crowds around her seemed to disappear, and she knew for that moment *she* was his only concern. Hearing Jesus' first word, her fear melted away.

"Daughter," he said, with such tenderness and kindness that she felt assured that she was loved and known by him.

"Daughter, your *faith* has made you well."

And suddenly it struck Reumah that it wasn't superstition about some magical piece of cloth that had healed her. Rather, it was her faith in this man – this Jesus, who was like no other she had ever met.

His captivating words held her gaze. 'Go in peace, and be free from your suffering.'

She didn't want to leave the ground where she was kneeling before Jesus. But as she watched Jesus turn back to speak to Jairus, Reumah realized that he had not only healed her and made that healing public; she knew that meeting Jesus had changed her life for ever.

At the side of the tightly packed street, she saw her husband standing with his arms opened wide, for the embrace they had both waited such a long time for. Looking lovingly at Dan as they walked the short distance home, she smiled: "My name is Reumah – no longer 'helpless' or 'unclean' – but 'exalted' – exalted by none other than Jesus!"

AD 1944–94

Bobula's eyes darted back and forth as she rushed along the jungle path. Every little noise made her jump! Her number two sister was crying as Bobula pulled her along behind; the branches of bushes slapping her in the face as she passed, causing the little girl's face to sting.

The sudden squawk of a parrot as it lifted off from a nearby tree coincided with a twig snapping under Bobula's foot! She screamed in terror, crouching low and pulling her little sister close.

"It's Mekai!" she whispered in her sister's ear. "He's come after me, just as Kimai said he would!"

Now both of them were crying, afraid to move in case the

evil spirit of the old man Mekai caught up with them. Bobula's cousin Kamai had teased her as she headed off to the family's bush house on her own for the first time.

"Watch out, Bobula!" the boy called out, laughing as he headed towards the river. "Mekai is lurking out there – he always did like banana trees!"

How she wished she hadn't called the old man names when an accident left him limping. Now Mekai was dead, and his spirit was living in the trees around the village. He would get his own back on her, for sure. Sitting low for a time, to hide from Mekai's spirit, Bobula's thoughts drifted from the boy's threats to the excitement of the day before. Brother number four had been born – only this time the tiny baby didn't die – and Bobula had stayed with the other women to see the baby come into the world.

"Bobula," her mother had said as she lay labouring, "you are nearly a woman and will soon have children of your own."

Bobula winced at the thought and hid behind her auntie's skirt, peeking through its grass layers to watch her mother give birth. Still a child herself, Bobula recoiled at what she saw. It all looked too painful for her liking, and brother number four was pale and wrinkly when he fell out on to their bark floor. And there was blood!

Her father had told her of the power of blood, and how touching it could bring death. The one dark room that was her home was filled with village women… waiting… waiting to see if brother number four was going to live or die… before anyone could touch him. He seemed to lie still for such a long time. Bobula peeked between her fingers to see what was going on, just as the slimy little bundle spluttered… and gasped… and cried! Then one of the women quickly pulled his shoulder up from the floor with a banana leaf, taking great care not to touch him with her fingers, and poured river water over him to wash away the blood that could bring bad luck or even death to the family.

Smiles and sounds of delight then brightened up the darkness, as the baby was finally put to his mother's breast, and word was sent to Bobula's father to tell him that at last he had a son to take hunting.

Now it was her mother's time of separation; she was not allowed outside her home until her bleeding stopped, in case she contaminated the men of the village. The family hadn't eaten for two days now because of brother number four, and Bobula's mother was unable to go into the forest in her normal role as gatherer for the family. Everyone was hungry.

"Bobula," her mother had said, a few hours earlier, "Bobula, you must go to the bush house and bring back some food. You are big enough to go without me; don't be afraid. Just remember to stop from time to time to allow your spirit to catch up with you. You don't want it to be left in the forest."

Hence Bobula's present predicament. It was entirely brother number four's fault! Yet she knew that soon she would have to do this job for a family of her own. She was very aware that her body was changing. Sometimes the boys teased her about it, and her cousin had recently been given in marriage to one of the village men. Soon it would be her turn. With those thoughts in her mind, she rose from the ground and bravely moved towards the jungle area where her family's food was growing.

Mekai didn't get her this time!

The old shack creaked and moved underfoot as the girls arrived. They needed a short rest before they gathered up the food to take back to the village. Soon the gentle sound of sleep filled the dirty little room.

Later, it wasn't the cockroaches climbing over their feet that woke them, but the rays of sunlight falling on their faces through the dilapidated leaf-thatched roof. Stretching herself into wakening, Bobula suddenly jumped. The sun was high in the Papuan sky and the girl realized that they needed to work hard if they were to gather food and get back along the tropical path before dusk. The little house seemed to sway on its stilts as they quickly ran down the steps. Bobula was convinced that the next heavy rains would wash it away. She must tell her father that they needed a new bush house. But for now food was the priority.

Bobula groaned as she looked over the vegetable patch she had planted with her mother a short time before. The whole area now looked like it had been attacked by vandals! The ground had been torn up, with holes replacing the neat rows of plants. Half-eaten sweet potatoes lay strewn around; little was left of the leafy green vegetable that was the staple food of the Siawi tribespeople. And Bobula knew exactly who the culprits were!

"Pigs!" Bobula shouted at her little sister. "The wild pigs have been back – they've eaten all our food! What will we do?"

The toddler stood gazing vaguely up at her sister, twisting her little necklace around her bony finger and shrugging her shoulders. Even at her age, she knew all about the wild pigs that roamed the area. They were big and vicious; always causing damage – but nice to eat – and their teeth made great beads! As the girls started to pick through what was left of the vegetables, a small flock of king parrots flew overhead, diverting their gaze from the ground. The beautiful red body plumage with a striking green band along its black wings brought a smile to the tiring children. The sight brought colour to a gloomy situation.

Bobula continued her gathering, finding a melon that hadn't been destroyed and a few papayas that had fallen to the ground. She was picking the wild tobacco leaves that she had promised to bring for her father when she caught sight of her sister eating a banana some ten feet away.

"Stop! Put it down! You know that tree does not belong to us. We are only allowed to eat from our own trees – father would be cross if he saw you stealing another's food!"

The child dropped the fruit in fright, and as soon as it hit the ground a large black rat ran out from the undergrowth, snatching it away. The complicated tribal laws were far beyond her understanding, but losing out to the rat made her cry. She loved bananas! Realizing she had frightened the little girl, Bobula reached out, giving her a reassuring hug, while encouraging her to help fill the cloths they had brought with them. It was time to go, before the sun disappeared altogether.

The journey back to the village seemed longer because of the weight of their load. Bobula's number two sister was only able to carry a small cloth filled with greens and tobacco that Bobula had tied to her naked little body. She in turn was laden down with heavier foods, but was happy that her gathering had been successful – up to a point. Soon, they heard the familiar sounds of dogs barking and babies crying. The village lay only a few yards ahead.

And Mekai must have been resting as they made their way through the trees and giant forest ferns, because he didn't bother her all the way home!

Most days in Siawi were filled with the simple business of staying alive. Hunger was a constant with this brave, resilient people, and so the battle against it was always foremost in their thoughts. They didn't know what day it was, or what month, or what year, for that matter. If you were strong enough, you could walk for two hours and reach the Sepik River, where the fishing was better. Some of the men had even taken journeys of two or three days to visit families at other villages, always careful to avoid tribes of different language groups, where violence could so easily erupt. Violence and hunger made strange bedfellows, and Bobula had heard stories of men who still practised cannibalism. The thought made her shudder, but she felt fairly safe, as she had never gone any further than the family bush hut – until one fateful day that would stay in her mind for ever.

The men of the tribe were sitting around the fire, smoking bush tobacco and deciding when the next pig hunt should be, when their conversation turned to some of the young women of the village. A few of the girls were ready to have husbands, and a discussion ensued on who should be given to whom. Bobula's uncle spoke up, saying that he had a cousin in a neighbouring village who needed a wife, and that Bobula should be the one to go. As tradition had it, Bobula's father had no say in the matter, and the men of the village decided that she would leave the next day for the three-hour walk, to be the child-bride of a man who was nearly as old as her father.

Next morning, the sun was barely up as Bobula said a

tearful goodbye to her mother; unsure if she would ever see her again. Number two sister clung to her leg, crying, while baby brother number four smiled at her, not knowing what all the fuss was about. The only comforting thought was that her "agemate" Meni was going with her. Born around the same time, they had been friends for always, and Meni too had been promised as a wife for one of the men in the same village. Bobula's uncle and father led the way as the girls lagged behind, trying to be brave, but very unsure as to what the future held for them.

At least Mekai would never be able to find her now!

The journey was a long and tedious one, through tropical forest paths which were occasionally brightened by a beautiful pink orchid pushing through the heavy green foliage. The temperature was soaring and the humidity high, requiring them to stop frequently for rest, and to ensure that their spirits had time to catch up with them in this unfamiliar territory. The girls noticed that sections of the path they were travelling hadn't been used much, and at times they wondered if they were lost. But the men walked ahead confidently, boasting of great hunting trips through this part of the forest. Each man's victory story was grander than the others, and the girls giggled at the foolishness of it all. Then, just as they heard thunder in the distance, the little party passed a few bush huts beside planted gardens and a number of fruit trees.

"The village must be close now," Bobula whispered to Meni, wondering how she would ever get to know which of these trees she would be allowed to pick from!

A few women passed them on the path, hesitant at first, then smiling a greeting when they realized they were fellow tribesmen. Then, almost without warning, the path opened out into a clearing at the edge of the village that was to become Bobula's lifelong home. A tonal sing-song greeting was called out by Bobula's uncle, and in no time a group of men came towards them. The men moved off to talk, while the girls were left sitting on the ground to wait.

Bobula and Meni looked around nervously; it didn't take long for them to realize that this village was very similar to their own. The houses were all built on one side of a small river. There seemed to be quite a lot of them, all set on stilts five to six feet off the ground to avoid being washed away if the river ever burst its banks, or if the evil spirits tried to stab you through the bark floor while you were sleeping. Most of them looked sturdy enough; the girls could see the women sitting on their porches, talking, smoking and pointing in their direction. A young pig was squealing for all it was worth as small children and a dog were chasing it around the village fire. Boys around their own age were dancing beside the river, appeasing the river spirits before they ventured in after the little fish which might provide supper, if they managed to catch them.

Yes, it all looked very much like home – apart from one thing – it wasn't!

"Bobula! Buko!"

Bobula's father sang out to her to come to him – and the girl froze.

"Bobula! Buko!" he repeated impatiently.

Bobula got to her feet, moving slowly towards him, her head bowed low. She knew there was nothing she could do about the situation. Every girl had to have a husband sometime

– but usually they knew the man beforehand. Now, three hours' walk away from home, and not yet feeling like a woman, she was to be given to a man she did not know, and when her father left she would be alone with strangers. She felt helpless.

Stiff with fear, Bobula felt a man's hand lift up her chin. Looking her up and down, he walked around her to view this woman who had been brought from the neighbouring village. Eventually a smile crossed his face, and he announced that he would accept Bobula as his wife. Her father and uncle seemed pleased with their day's work and went off to eat with the village elders. The man who was to be Bobula's husband pointed in the direction of a house and then followed after the men. As Bobula walked towards her new home, she looked for her "age-mate" Meni and saw her disappear up the steps of another house, not too far away. Her legs felt like river stones as she reluctantly tried to pull them up the rough wooden steps towards the woman sitting on the porch.

"Make sure you are a good wife to Wourinau," the woman said sternly. "He is my number two son – the only one left alive."

Bobula heard a baby cry as she went to sit on the porch beside her mother-in-law.

"That is my daughter's child. She is in separation at the minute. Go and see if she needs anything."

Bobula went inside the dark room to meet her sister-in-law and the new baby. She was glad of the darkness, as unwelcome tears spilled over, leaving tracks on her dusty cheeks. The new mother had heard all that had gone on outside, and Bobula was touched by her softly spoken words.

"Don't worry, young one," she said. "Mother just wants you to know who is boss. She'll be glad you are here to take Wourinau off her hands. She's gathered for him for too many years – it's time he had a wife, and he'll be good to you. He really is a kind man. Now come and hold the baby, while I slip out the back."

Bobula relaxed a little as she held the tiny baby in her arms. Soon she would become firm friends with her sister-in-law, relying on her guidance in this strange place.

Then, as darkness fell, Bobula's fear returned; in the corner of the smoky, smelly room – with all Wourinau's family gathered in for the night – Bobula became a wife.

During the day there was so much to do, especially in a strange place. Bobula not only had to get to know people – especially the members of her new family – but also which part of the forest belonged to them. She had to learn which trees she could pick from and which land was hers to cultivate. It was good to keep busy; that way, she didn't spend so much time thinking about home. Having her friend Meni in the village with her was wonderful. They tried to plan their gathering trips at the same time, and they would link arms and walk, talk, and giggle together as they made their way down paths which were gradually becoming more familiar to them.

One day as they returned to the village, they could see some of the men chopping up a tree, the sharpened stone axe-head eating its way easily into the wood. And there was Wourinau right in the middle of things, giving orders. They didn't appear to be merely chopping firewood, so Bobula sang out a greeting to her husband, enquiring what they were doing. With a big smile on his face, Wourinau replied: "I'm building my new wife a house of her own!"

For the first time since she had left her family, Bobula felt a surge of delight. Wourinau was indeed a kind man, just as his sister had said, and as she watched him build their little house, with the porch facing the river, she found it hard to believe the stories he had told her of his earlier cannibal practices! Perhaps one day she would fill his home with sons – but not yet, she hoped; the vision of her mother's last labour was still an unpleasant memory.

Time is a strange concept in Siawi. There are no clocks; no calendars; no seasons. The sun comes up in the morning and disappears, leaving darkness, in the evening. That means there is no age. No one has a birthday, so no one knows how old they are. You are either young or old; there is nothing in between. Village history is usually categorized by the big events: storms, flooding, tribal war – or plagues. At times Bobula saw the village population reduced by as much as twenty per cent, when illness spread through each home like wildfire.

But the real enemy was fear: fear of the sorcery that caused the sickness, and terror at so many deaths, adding to the number of evil spirits who needed to be appeased. Friends in life became enemies in death. The sun in the sky may have delivered nature's light, but it was the darkness of the spirit world that ruled their lives, rendering them helpless.

Years had passed, but Bobula was still young. Her first house had been rebuilt twice because of flooding, and by this time she had wrapped two sons in banana leaves and sadly buried them in the ground close to the edge of the village. The scrawny infants hadn't breathed after they had fallen out on the floor, and so the women had left them to die, unwilling to risk the curse of the blood to come to their aid.

"If they were meant to live, they would have breathed by themselves," or so the older women of the village had told Bobula.

At least she was better off than her age-mate. Her dear friend had had twins, the worst thing that could happen to any woman. Two of anything was bad luck; but two babies at once was really a bad omen, not just for her but for the whole village! Bobula watched in silence as the girl twin was taken to the edge of the village and left to die, while Meni nursed her son in a dark room filled with sadness and fear.

The men had been gone for a few days when Bobula went into labour for a third time. They had been preparing for days to go hunting. New bows were made, arrows sharpened, and the young boys had been play-acting out the adventure ahead with bravado. Only a few old, sick men and young boys were left behind with the women. Two days into the hunt, in a smoke-filled room, Bobula laboured quietly, wondering if on this occasion the spirits would allow her to have a live child.

The contractions were coming one on top of the other, and a young girl was sent to get a little container of water from the river, to be ready to wash the baby – if it lived. As Bobula pushed to expel the pain, as much as the baby inside her, she felt a sudden plop on the floor!

"It's yamae!" Meni shouted; a girl!

The women stepped back from the helpless infant, waiting without a word. Bobula watched and saw her little daughter struggle, her dark curls sticky against her tiny head, bloody mucus streaking the loose folds of skin that covered her fragile form. More than anything in the world, Bobula wished – no, longed – that she could do something to help her! But she couldn't! The baby would have to choose either to live or die – all by herself.

It felt as if time had stood still, and Bobula was about to wail in grief when she heard the most beautiful sound a mother could hear – her baby crying! Meni rushed forward to wash off the curse-causing blood, and for the first time Bobula held her very own baby in her arms.

"Wourinau will be pleased," she said to her mother-in-law; "he is a father at last."

"Not the son he wanted," was the reply, "but a daughter to gather for him when you are old."

Bobula was too tired to pay any attention to the sting in her mother-in-law's words. She cuddled her lovely daughter close on the hard wooden floor, unaware of the joy this child would bring her in the years to come.

There were no more live children for Bobula. Opa, however, was a good daughter and a healthy one. Like others in the village, she had her fair share of malaria, but managed to survive the perils of village life as she was growing up. Now, Bobula could see womanhood make its approaches to her only child, and she knew that soon Opa would be given as a wife –

and the circle would begin all over again. Nothing ever changed in Siawi.

Then one day Bobula and Opa were returning from the bush hut. Opa's yamau was riding on her shoulders, a happy little boy, while the two women carried bananas and papayas in cloths tied around their shoulders. Just before they reached the village, a strange noise came from the sky. Looking up, they saw an unusual "something" flying above them, with strange markings written across it. Terrified, the two women dived for the cover of nearby bushes, Opa's yamau falling from her shoulders into the vegetation!

"What was that?" Bobula asked her startled daughter, as they tried to comfort the child, rubbing his skinned limbs.

"Looks like bad magic to me," was Opa's rather puzzled reply.

Gathering themselves together, the two women ran for the village, only to find more anxious faces – and no answer as to what they had seen. The sight was talked about for many days, but it was only some time later, when two of the men returned from the Green River Trading Post two days distant, that news was brought concerning the strange object.

It was called an aeroplane! People ran from all over the village to hear about the strange long box that had wings to make it fly in the sky. Men could sit in it and be taken long journeys over the forest. The discussion went on for hours. Bobula thought the men had been drinking some bad water and had gone mad!

Boxes that could fly like birds – big enough to hold people!

She had heard enough and went back to her porch to smoke some bush tobacco – at least she knew that was real! But the talk around the fire that night, and for many more to come, was of the aeroplane, and what it had brought: Wesiwesis – white people. Missionaries – people who brought "God's talk" and medicine to take away sickness. They were living with a tribe three days' walk away, called the Ama people. Bobula pretended that she wasn't interested, but she lay awake at night listening to her son-in-law Kawi tell Opa of the men's discussions at the village meetings.

"Do you think the Wesiwesis could come here, Kawi?"

"I don't know, Opa; the Tultul is afraid that maybe they will harm the village."

"Go to sleep!" grunted Wourinau from across the room, "it's all just talk – the Wesiwesis don't care about us."

And as Bobula turned towards the wall, she had no idea of how much things would change in the next ten years.

Opa was worried. Her mother was ill yet again. She coughed and coughed and wasn't interested in eating. She was skinnier than the dogs that roamed the village, and Opa didn't know what to do to help her. How she wished that the missionaries would come, as the Siawi people had requested so many years ago. They might have medicine to make her mother well.

Ten years earlier, the village elders, including her father, walked the three days' journey to speak to the missionaries with the Ama tribe. They asked for missionaries to be sent to Siawi, and on their return they even started to clear a patch of ground, in case they came. Opa had two more children by this time – and still they waited. But there were rumours circulating that the missionaries were going to visit soon and hold discussions with the village elders in Siawi itself. Things were looking up.

Weeks passed, and Bobula had recovered from her latest chest illness. She was no longer able to go into the bush gathering, but continued to help Opa with the cooking. One day, a loud "throp, throp" noise came out of the sky. It was like nothing they had ever heard before. The villagers ran out of their houses, fearing a huge storm was about to rip their homes out of the ground. Suddenly a metal machine appeared to fall out of the sky, blowing debris all over the place. As it set down on large flat feet on the small clearing at the other side of the river, Bobula and Opa grabbed the children and ran for cover in the bush with the other women. The men bravely stood their ground, watching the whirling wings above the strange flying monster slow and finally come to a stop.

Fear, excitement and curiosity caused Bobula's heart to beat faster. Some of the children were crying and all the women were talking at once! When the awful noise stopped, they stepped forward a short distance to see what was happening. Curiosity had won! Closer and closer they came, as they saw three men jump down from the flying machine. They could see from that distance that they had white skin.

"It's the missionaries, Mother. They've come!"

A big smile crossed Opa's face, as she encouraged the other women to move back into the village to see what was happening.

"Wesiwesis!" Bobula grunted, treating the whole matter with suspicion.

But the truth was, she was just as keen as everyone else to see what the men "from far away" looked like. *Ugly*... was her first impression. They were tall, easily head and shoulders above the tallest of their men. Their skin was paler than she had imagined, and they had pink ears! But it was their noses that looked so strange – they stuck out so far from their faces. Bobula instantly decided that she was glad that her man didn't look like that!

Once she was brave enough to get even closer, Bobula noticed that the men had eyes as blue as the sky and hair nearly as fair as their skin. Soon everyone was asking questions at once, but the visitors couldn't understand what they were saying. Meni joked with her friend that these men had no feet, as she couldn't see any toes with the strange coverings that they wore!

Bobula threw her head back and laughed.

It was a happy sight. The Wesiwesis smiled at everyone and stood graciously while people poked and prodded them, totally unconcerned by the crowd's investigations. After a little while the village elders shooed the women and children away and the serious business began.

Bobula and Opa sat on their porch, smoking feverishly and wishing that they had bigger ears to hear what was being said. The talking went on for some time. The visitors could speak Melanesian pidgin, and a few of the more travelled men of the village translated what they could understand. Then they walked across the river, and Bobula could see the Wesiwesis waving their hands around the area, pointing here and there.

Soon they were back in the noisy machine and up in the air, before the women could get over the river to see them go.

"The missionaries have agreed to come to our village!" the Tultul announced that night around the fire. Never had Bobula seen the village leader with such a big grin on his face; but it was hard for him to keep order, with everyone talking at once. With time, he was able to explain that each of the tribesmen had agreed to give a little piece of land on the other side of the river to build an airstrip. The Wesiwesi men would come first and build small huts for their families. They would also pay the men for helping to clear the land so that an aeroplane could land.

"They have promised to pay us with machetes, lamps, cooking pots and other things to help us," the Tultul continued. "And they will learn our language to tell us of 'God's talk', and bring medicine for the sick."

The consensus of the village was very positive, especially from the younger members of the tribe. Wourinau and Bobula said little. Time would tell if the missionaries would keep their word and return. But return they did.

For the next nine months the village was a mass of activity while the ground was cleared for the airstrip. The Siawi, who had been used to planning their own agenda at a more leisurely pace, at first found it difficult to follow the instructions of the two missionaries. The Wesiwesis were so fussy about everything. Every little bump had to be levelled, and once that was done, the grass had to be kept short. Then there were the huts to build – a few to live in and one to use as the village medical centre. From Bobula's porch, the landscape across the river was beginning to look completely different.

Excitement was building. The two men had left the village a short time earlier, telling the people that when they returned they would be coming back with their families – to stay. Instructions had been given that when the little plane circled overhead they were to make sure everyone was well away from the airstrip, so that the plane could land without injuring anyone.

One morning a sing-song call was heard throughout the entire village.

"The plane is coming – I hear the plane!"

People came from everywhere. Women grabbed children, holding them tightly as the plane circled overhead. They cheered in nervous expectation as the white "box with wings" landed on Siawi's very own airstrip. Holding back for just a few minutes, the women and children surged forward as the two white women and five small children stepped onto Siawi soil for the first time. Bobula stroked and poked them, amazed at the sight of the little children, whose hair was whiter than anything she had ever seen before! She smiled at the missionaries' wives, thinking of the first time she had come to the village so many years ago, and wondered if they missed home as she had done. But all she got in return were smiles; the newcomers really did seem happy to be with them!

After the missionaries moved in, Bobula and Meni spent their days sitting on their porches watching what the white women were doing on the other side of the river. They were strange people. They wore clothes from their neck down and even coverings for their feet; and they always seemed to be washing things – especially their children! The construction of bigger houses for the missionaries and their children to live in created lots of discussion between the two friends, especially the holes cut in the side-walls to let the light in! But the Wesiwesi ladies were friendly; every afternoon they would come and sit on the porch, and learn to speak a little more of their language. What seemed so easy to pronounce for Bobula and Meni was a lot more work for the new girls in the village; but they persevered, with lots of laughs along the way!

Bobula noticed that neither of the missionary ladies liked to see any of the villagers sick. They would even risk the evil spirits that roamed in the village at night in order to visit someone who needed medicine after the sun had gone down. Bobula hated medicine! Sometimes, when she had a fever or when the coughing sickness returned, her daughter would insist that she go to the village health centre, but she would hide her tablet in her skirt when the missionary's head was turned! Then, before you knew it, she was sick again! So an unspoken rule was made that someone had to witness Bobula actually swallowing her medicine, before she was allowed to go back to her house.

Early every morning, the villagers heard the sound of the conch shell to let them know that the medical centre was open. Many lives were saved because of quick treatment for ailments that would have been fatal before the missionaries came. Even though Bobula recognized this, she still hated taking medicine, but soon she realized a crafty little trick that benefited her both ways. The missionaries always had little items of foodstuffs that Bobula loved to get her hands on. Knowing how upset they were when she wouldn't take her medicine, Bobula would resort to bribery.

"If you give me this little tin of fish… or a little salt… or a little grease, then I'll swallow my tablet with it!"

So the decline in Bobula's health slowed somewhat, making everyone happy.

Meanwhile, the men of the village were busy building again. This time it was the biggest house Bobula had ever seen!

"Are more Wesiwesis coming, Kawi?" Bobula asked as they settled down on the floor for the night. "That's a very big house you are building."

"No, Bobula. It's a house for the Wesiwesis to teach us 'God's talk' and how to read and write. The house is for everyone in the village, not for the Wesiwesis."

Bobula had waited many years to hear "God's talk", and as she drifted off to sleep she wondered if she would still be alive when the missionaries knew enough words to be able to tell her. Across the little river, the missionaries wondered the very same thing.

For a whole year, the Siawi waited for the Wesiwesis to return from their visit back to their own homeland. It had been a hard year. While the missionaries were away, Bobula had lost the two most precious people in her life. Her husband of many years had died, as old men do. But it was the death of Meni that had shocked Bobula even more severely. A sudden fever, and no available medicine, had taken the life of her dear friend and sharer of her memories. The pain in her heart was unbearable, and the wail of her grief joined that of the whole village in the most desolate sound ever to leave human lips. The wailing went on into the night, and the helplessness of their plight was heard in heaven – for Meni had died before she had been able to hear "God's talk".

The place was literally buzzing! The men sat on the benches at the back of the large village house, while the women and children sat on the floor in front of them. It was still only shortly after daybreak, but today was the day both the Siawi and the missionaries had been waiting for. Today would start the teaching of "God's talk"! Five years had passed since the missionaries had first made contact at the invitation of the village elders. They had spent much time learning the language, putting "God's talk" into Siawi words as accurately as possible. Day after day, the people had benefited from their medical care. Now they had been invited to come to hear what the Wesiwesis had come for, all along – "God's talk". No one had been forced or coerced, yet every single person from the tribe came to hear.

Bobula sat with Opa and listened firstly as to how "God's talk" came to be, and that it wasn't a "white man's" Bible, as she had thought. In fact, she learnt that the writers were olive-skinned people. Day after day, the old woman heard the story of the battle in heaven between God and Satan; how God had then created the earth, wanting Adam and Eve to be his friends; how people had then decided to do what they themselves wanted and turned away from God, because of God's enemy Satan. Bobula was surprised and delighted that for many, many years

God kept speaking to his people and telling them that one day a saviour would come, who would make it possible to be friends with God once more. Sometimes she tutted, when the people were foolish and didn't do as God asked them. Then stories of great heroes in "God's talk" made the people laugh and cheer, giving them lots to discuss throughout the day.

Often, Bobula listened to the teaching again in the evening, on a little wind-up recorder that Opa and Kawi borrowed from the missionaries. And as she listened to the strange machine that could steal your voice, Bobula occasionally wondered what Meni would have made of it all.

Normal life continued in Siawi. Food still had to be gathered, pigs had to be hunted; but before that, every day, the people came to hear more of the wonderful story of God.

You could have heard a pin drop the day that Bobula heard that God had sent his own "Imau" from heaven to earth – his own firstborn Son! Jesus was wonderful! Bobula heard about the stories he told and the people he healed and the lives he changed. But delight turned to horror when she heard that evil men took God's one and only Son and killed him, by nailing him to a cross! Tears ran down many faces that day; but then the missionaries explained that it was all in God's plan, because blood had to be shed in order that the evil in men's hearts could be taken away. It was the only way to become God's friend: to accept the sacrifice of his Son to take away the evil in your heart that kept him and you apart, and to allow him to live inside you, not by an evil spirit, but by God the Holy Spirit.

Bobula found it hard to understand at first. Opa and Kawi had each gone to speak to the missionaries and had returned to the house as Christians! Bobula saw the difference in their lives – the happiness they now had because Jesus was in their hearts – but she didn't quite get it all. Meanwhile, her coughing sickness had returned and she was growing weaker. How she wished she could understand "God's talk" better.

Listening the second time round, as the missionaries went over the teaching again, Bobula suddenly sat bolt upright, as if a light had been switched on in her head! All her life, she had believed that there was power – evil power – in blood. Yet now she understood that there was power in Jesus' blood, as it spilled into the ground for her! Not evil power, but power that came from God to take away the wrongdoing in her life; power to make her God's friend – no, better than that – God's child! Jesus' blood was not to make her afraid – it was to make her a new person!

Later that day, as she explained all this to the missionary, there was no doubt that Bobula understood at last and had begun a new life with Jesus. Never again would she feel afraid; never again would she stop on the path to wait for her spirit to catch up with her; never again would she fear the sorcerer's spell; never again would she be helpless. Her help for now and hope for the future was all found in the one who lived in her heart – Jesus.

The months passed, and Bobula was growing older and weaker. Peace, not fear, was written across her face, even though she knew that soon she would make the last great journey beyond her village. The dogs were barking on the ground below, and the cicadas were chirping in the trees above, as a little group of women gathered on Opa's porch. It was time to say goodbye to Bobula, her little frame barely a wriggle of bones now. Her head was resting on the lap of the lady missionary, who had grown to love her and who had fought to keep her healthy until she could hear "God's talk". No wailing anticipated her passing, but rather they sang to her songs of the God who had given his own "Imau" in order that Bobula could know him in the life to come.

Opa stroked her mother's little face, encouraging her to enjoy heaven and to remember that one day she would join her in God's wonderful home – for ever! As the sound of life became silent in Bobula's body, there was no lost wailing to announce her death, because Opa and many others had learnt the truth of the apostle Paul's words when he said that Christians don't sorrow as others who have no hope. Instead, they sat quietly; the only sound in their imaginings was of the angels' rejoicing as Bobula was welcomed into her eternal home.

The first Siawi believer had entered heaven's gates.

About "Helpless"

c. AD 32

Read for yourself the story of the haemorrhaging woman, as it is found in Mark's Gospel, chapter 5:21–34.

Other relevant biblical references:

Old Testament teaching on women with irregular female bleeding – Leviticus 15:19–30.

AD 1944–94

Bobula's story was told to me by a dear missionary friend, Liz Cuthbert. Liz and her husband Matthew worked with the New Tribes Mission for many years in the Sepik region of Papua New Guinea, among the Siawi people. (They are now the local representatives of NTM in Ireland.)

I am deeply grateful to Liz for giving me the privilege of telling Bobula's story. It is with excitement that I look forward to the day when I shall worship with Bobula at heaven's throne.

Powerless

C. AD 32

Alexander froze in fear, as the ground shook beneath his bare feet!

"Alexander! Did you feel that?" his young companion shouted from behind.

Alexander rose quickly from the soft, loose earth of their homemade long-jump pit. All around him, tall stalks topped with golden grain obscured the boy's view. Dusting the dirt from his body, he stretched to full height to look over the field of corn that was almost ready to harvest.

A rhythmical thud, thud, thud could be heard, causing the ground to vibrate. The boys faked bravery to each other, while their hearts beat faster and their imaginations ran away with fanciful thoughts of mythical creatures coming to get them.

"Perhaps your uncle has sent a dragon to punish us for digging up his field for our games, Alexander."

"Aw, don't be silly – he doesn't even know we're here," Alexander replied, hoping his young accomplice believed the words more than he did.

As the disturbing noise grew louder, curiosity got the better of the two young athletes and they started to make their way through the corn to see where their adventure might take them. Suddenly, a little fieldmouse, disturbed from its feasting, landed on Alexander's head, sending the boys sprinting, arms flying everywhere! They didn't stop running until they reached the road that cut through his uncle's farm! Then, rolling in laughter by the side of the road at the foolishness of their rodent encounter, the boys saw an imposing sight coming towards them.

"Quickly, Alexander! Hide! It's the Romans!"

Alexander didn't need any further coaxing, as he and his friend rolled back into the corn, commanding a grandstand view of the approaching Roman legion. On the road the boys saw row after row of Roman soldiers, stretching into the distance as far as the eye could see. The thud of six thousand pairs of hobnailed sandals marching in time on the stone-built Roman road caused the ground around them to shudder under their fearsome might.

At the front of the mighty army, coming ever closer, the boys recognized the badge of Rome: the mighty eagle, carried proudly by the *aquilifer*, seated high on the back of a fine brown steed. Alexander covered his ears, as first the standard bearer and then some one hundred and twenty horses of the cavalry unit passed by, just feet from where he was hiding. Swirling dust, disturbed by the horses' hooves passing, made the boys cough and splutter; their eyes stung with the irritating debris flying around them. But fear prevented their escape from the unpleasantness.

"It must be a whole legion, Alexander! Have you ever seen so many soldiers? I wonder where they are going?"

"Sshh, they might hear us and take us prisoner!"

"They can't do that, Alexander – we're Greeks. My father says that we are the friends of the Romans."

"Well, I wouldn't like to find out. Look at that big centurion! He must be at least six feet tall. Any of those hundred men behind him will do exactly as he says – without question!"

The boys continued their unexpected lesson on the Roman military, as the mass of trained soldiers kept coming. The spectacle before them confirmed that there was no army in the world to match the might of Rome. Each individual soldier wore a bronze helmet, which included a neck protector and hinged cheekpieces. Over a short woollen tunic, his body was protected by body armour made with strips of metal secured by leather cords, and on his feet were the hobnailed leather sandals that thudded as he marched, while only the centurions wore metal greaves to protect their legs.

"Hey, Alexander, look at the size of that sword swinging from his waist! It must be two feet long! I wouldn't like to fight against him!"

"You wouldn't stand a chance," Alexander replied. "His shield is so big that you would never get near him. Anyway, he would probably stick you with his spear long before that – just like this!"

Alexander rolled over his friend in playful fight, the pair deciding that a Roman battle was far more fun than Greek philosophy. But by the time they decided to work on a truce, the legion was still passing by.

"Seriously, Alexander, where do you think the legion is heading?"

"Probably to guard the eastern borders of the Empire. My

uncle says that the Parthians are always causing the Romans trouble. They want nothing to do with 'Pax Romana'!" he said gruffly, mimicking his uncle.

Chuckling, the boys decided they'd seen enough and headed back through the cornfields towards home. As ever, adventures are easily brought to an end by the call of one's stomach – especially if that stomach belongs to a growing lad. The distance to Gerasa was covered quickly, as they talked of fierce legions, whose very name mentally conjured up huge numbers and oppressive strength. And yet the boys' Greek nature reasoned that, without the Romans, they would not have the lovely town of Gerasa to live in, with its two fine theatres and splendid Greco-Roman architecture.

As they walked, Alexander remarked how much better it was to live on this side of the Sea of Galilee, in the beautiful fertile region of Decapolis, than on the other side, with the Jews, and all that that meant. And so the busy afternoon of athletics, battle and philosophy ended, as the two weary boys made their way through the column-flanked street in anticipation of supper. As they parted, Alexander was envious of his friend, who would, no doubt, recount the adventures of the day to his father. How he wished that he could do the same!

Reclining beside the low table, Alexander reached forward to dip his bread into the dish of olive oil. Before it had reached his mouth, his uncle started to speak.

"Alexander, you won't be at school for the next week. It's our turn for harvest. All the men are gathering in our fields tomorrow at dawn, and since your father has left me to work the whole farm alone, I think it's time that you earned your keep.

You'll be in the fields with the rest of us, boy, instead of sitting in the classroom filling your head with nonsense!"

Before he had time to reply, Alexander's aunt shouted at her husband for his careless remarks: "It's not the boy's fault that your brother has turned into a madman! Leave him alone!"

"He's not a madman!" the horrified youngster cried, jumping up from the table and knocking the food over in his rush to leave. "It's demons, I tell you – demons! My father can't help the way he is! He's not a madman… he's not… he's not!"

Alexander ran like the wind, through the streets, over the fields and on and on, for how long he didn't know. When cramp eventually stopped his flight, he fell into the long grass with sobbing cries and heaving shoulders. The past months had been like a recurring nightmare, playing over and over again, in his waking as well as his sleeping moments. His father had been a hard-working man, sharing the responsibility of the family farm with his younger brother, Calix. Alexander loved his father dearly, especially as his mother had died when he was very young, leaving them both to care for each other. Everything was going very well with the farm and with Alexander's schooling, until one day that he could never forget.

His father had become uncharacteristically irritable and easily annoyed. He began going out late at night, leaving Alexander in the care of his recently married brother.

No one knew where he went or what he was doing in those late-night forays. But, each time he returned, Alexander felt that his father had lost a little piece of himself. First to go were his warm, inviting smiles; then his kind words. Soon, he stopped asking Alexander about his games and his school work, and –

more painfully – they never talked about Alexander's mother any more. Their home became a place of quiet loneliness, the silence interrupted only by occasional outbursts of unrestrained anger from the man Alexander could no longer recognize as his father. And yet he still loved him.

Alexander quickly learnt when it was time to hide from his father, ducking when a stray pot was sent spinning in his direction. The outbursts were becoming more regular, his anger more out of control. There were times when Alexander looked into his father's eyes and couldn't see behind the rage and confusion. At those times Alexander was convinced that someone – or something – other than his father was looking back at him.

The day his father went away started just like any other. Calix's wife had made breakfast, and Alexander was wrapping up his piece of goat's cheese in a cloth to take to school. Suddenly they heard a disturbance coming from the street outside. Some women were squealing, and there was an indescribable growling noise piercing the air. Uncle Calix and Alexander reached the door first, horrified at the sight that met them.

There, right in front of them, was Alexander's father, swinging around the pillars, screaming, out of his mind – and stark naked! Blood was coming from gashes in his skin. His eyes flashed in rage. He was like a man possessed.

Women ran through the streets, picking up their children as they went, terrified of someone they could only describe as a monster! Alexander witnessed men running at his father from all directions, trying to restrain him as he tossed aside everything, and everyone, in his path.

"Stop, Father! Stop!" he cried, but to no avail, as he ran after this demented specimen of humanity.

Then, from out of nowhere, a net landed on top of the man, trapping him like an injured animal. As Alexander watched, his beloved father was tied with ropes and metal shackles bound his feet, and for the briefest of times he seemed to sink to the ground in despair. It was then that Alexander saw it: behind the blackness of his father's eyes, he saw terror – terror at no longer being able to control his body, or his life. He looked utterly powerless.

As Alexander reached out to touch the man who was his idol, all hell broke loose. With an other-worldly power and a gut-wrenching scream, his father rose to his feet, bursting his chains and shackles as if they had been thread. The voices coming from his mouth belonged to others – many others. It was as if an army – no, a legion – of evil forces had invaded the body of the man who used to tell him bedtime stories, swing him in his arms and make him feel safe. And Alexander knew that somewhere deep inside this being was his father.

Alexander could do nothing but watch, as the man ran out of the town, far away from home and far away from his son.

Now, months after that event, lying under an oak tree miles from home, Alexander couldn't get the pictures out of his mind. The boy, now approaching manhood, was tortured by memories – longing that the nightmare would end and his father would come home.

"Father, Father! Where are you?" he shouted in anguish.

"I miss you so much! She had no right to call you a madman – you're not a madman!"

Yet Alexander knew that the alternative was almost as shocking – a demoniac! His father – controlled by unclean spirits. He didn't know how, but he knew it must be true. Yet, if there was some way that he could be delivered, then the boy was sure that one day his father could return to him. He refused to give up hope.

As his sobbing settled, Alexander reminisced over his trip to market the previous month to buy fish for his aunt. A Jewish fisherman came to Gerasa regularly to sell his catch at the town's market. The town centre was busy that day, as Alexander stood in line. The fisherman looked a bit pale and fraught on that occasion and Alexander listened in on the conversation he was having with some ladies.

"I'm going to have to rethink coming here if the authorities don't do something about those demoniacs who live in the caves around the harbour close to Gadara!" he remonstrated. "They are becoming more violent – and indecent," he spluttered. "Why, they ran after me today – all the way up the hill! I don't know what would have happened if those swineherds hadn't come to my aid!"

"Swineherds!" the women laughed. "Imagine a Jew being rescued by pig breeders!"

"You may laugh," the fisherman continued, "but the country seems to be filled with the demon-possessed these days. There's something going on, I tell you! Mark my words! It wouldn't surprise me if there was another war going on in the heavens – just like before the world was created – and..."

"There are always battles going on in the underworld!" one of the ladies snorted in disgust. "You Jews take it all too seriously. You need more gods, like us Greeks. How is your one god going to take on the underworld?"

Soon, the remaining customers became weary of the conversation, complaining about being kept waiting. But Alexander wanted to hear more.

"What happened, sir?" he asked when his turn finally came.

"What are you talking about, boy?"

"What happened just before the world was created?"

"Oh, that!" the fisherman replied impatiently, as his conversation had moved on by this time. "Well, son, there was a dreadful battle for control in heaven between God and Satan, who was once an angel of light. God won, of course, but Satan was banished to earth, with all his demons – legions of them! They always cause trouble, but lately they have been more active than usual – tormenting people in dreadful ways. There's something going on, I tell you; something!"

"C'mon Jew, move on! Stop filling the lad's head with the foolish talk of your religion."

Demons – legions of them!

That afternoon, Alexander let the man's words roll over in his mind again, as he slipped the piece of soggy bread out of his pocket and into his mouth. The disagreement with his aunt and uncle would have to be put behind him; soon he would have to make his way home. Helping with the harvest wasn't a problem; but he refused to allow anyone to talk about his father as a madman! And as he looked into the distance towards the sea, he wondered if one of the demoniacs the fisherman had encountered in the country of the Gadarenes last month could have been his father. Even if that were so, he felt powerless to do anything about it.

The man they called Legion beat his chest with clenched fists, forcing out another tormented scream. The sky may have been blue as he looked over the Sea of Galilee from the hillside of Gadara, but the colour black was all he ever saw. The sun didn't shine in his sky.

In an effort to expel the horrors that raged within him, he lifted a piece of flint from the loose rocks, slicing his naked chest. It did no good. The horrors remained, enmeshed in the very fabric of his being. The voices in his head thumped with an agonizing pain, forcing him to do as they said, tormenting his reason, which was harder to find with each passing day. Memories of how he came to be living in the place of the dead were filed so far back in his memory that he found them well-nigh impossible to recall. In the briefest moments of clarity, he saw the face of a boy flash across his mind. Who was he? Legion didn't know, yet every time he saw the image, a cry came from a different place within him – a place Legion felt was the real him.

Growling at the pigs feeding on acorns in the surrounding oak grove, Legion felt jealous of them. They may have had their snouts in the dirt, but even they experienced some control over where they walked and what they ate. Their masters, the swineherds, looked after them better than his masters did. He was constantly hungry; constantly in pain; constantly angry and constantly powerless to do anything about it.

Those whose tombs he shared for sleeping called him to death, but his masters wouldn't even let him go there. And the swineherds working nearby could never know the torment behind his screams. He truly was a man possessed.

As Legion looked across to the other side of the lake, his possessors pulled him from the gaze. There was someone – or something – they didn't like, or even feared, across those waters, on the Jewish side of the Jordan Valley. As he agonized in the dusk, menacing clouds gathered overhead, prematurely darkening the scene. Fishing boats started to turn for shore – all except one. It kept on coming. As the wind strengthened, Legion headed for the tombs enclosed in the caves that lined the lakeside. Soon the wind was a gale; rain fell in torrents and the moon was blotted out by the blackest of clouds.

The waves on the Sea of Galilee were whipped into frenzied foam, like white horses riding on mountaintops, tossing the little boat to and fro. The ferocity of the storm was such that the sea threatened to swallow up ship and sailors alike; there could be no safe haven on that dreadful night of nights.

Legion watched from the shore, tearing at his skin, screaming the screams of the damned, somehow aware that he was about to face the greatest battle of his life. Suddenly – instantaneously – the sea was becalmed!

The waves fell flat; the clouds rolled back in the sky; the rain stopped; the gale stopped its howling. And the light of the moon shone once more on the little vessel, some miles out in the middle of the lake. In shock, Legion felt himself being pulled back into the darkness of the tombs, where he waited – for what, he didn't know.

There was no sleep to be had that night. Legion felt the atmosphere within him and around him thick with evil and panic; worse than anything he had ever felt before.

As the dawn started to push back the night skies, the tormented man crept out of the tombs, his head low to clear the cave entrance. Walking up the hill, he trembled, the air cool and clear against his skin after the storm of the previous night. Some distance below, in the small harbour, Legion watched the activity surrounding a small fishing boat. Fishermen with their tunics tucked up around their waists secured the vessel to the wooden pier with ropes.

He began to experience something new – fear. Until now, his life had been marked by anger, strength and violence, his possessors ensuring that everyone he encountered was afraid of him. Yet what remained of the real him sensed that they were afraid – of what, or whom, Legion did not know.

A battle of immense magnitude was raging inside his mortal frame. In a split second of time, Legion saw the cause of his tormentors' fear. It was the man who was stepping off the boat onto the shore. He was the one that hell had tried to drown in the storm the night before – the one whom Legion's possessors recognized immediately. And, deep inside his real self, Legion knew that the man on the boat had come through a storm just for him.

Wailing and screaming, Legion ran towards the little band

of men heading up the hill. Pushed to his knees by the many evil residents of his life, he heard the chief voice of his possessors cry out, naming the Man from the boat.

"What do you want with me, Jesus, Son of the Most High God?"

From a position of worship in front of the one before whom even the devils tremble, the demon paid homage to the one true and living God. Realizing that their rule of evil was finished, he tried to plead with Jesus, who had already commanded him to come out of the man.

"Swear to God that you won't torture me!" the demon implored, grovelling before the Creator of the universe.

As the encounter continued, Jesus asked the demon to name himself, so that the surrounding witnesses could see the magnitude of the situation. Horrified, the men gasped at the reply, stepping back in shock.

"My name is Legion," growled the voices coming from the destitute man, "for we are many!"

In an anguished display of torture and mayhem, a myriad of voices poured out of the one mouth, begging, pleading, entreating Jesus not to send them out of the area. Jesus was undoubtedly in control. The demons were now the ones who were powerless.

Close to this spiritual battle a herd of pigs was feeding. The swineherds, watching all that was going on, recognized that this man was one person who didn't need to be rescued by them from the demoniac who had been terrorizing the area. They stood transfixed, totally unaware of the shock that was soon to come their way.

Legion, knowing he must obey Jesus, looked for a better way of escape, with one last appeal to the judge of all the earth.

"Send us among the pigs; allow us to go into them," came the final plea.

Jesus granted their request. Those looking on cowered, as the man convulsed before them, the demons finally leaving his body at Jesus' command. The air around filled with their evil howling in the few seconds that it took for them to reach the herd of swine. Never before had such a noise echoed through Gadara.

Squealing in terror, two thousand pigs ran around in frantic panic. The swineherds could do nothing but get out of their way, as the animals rushed headlong down the steep bank and into the lake, drowning in its cool waters!

And Legion sat in stillness at the feet of Jesus.

Alexander wiped the sweat from his brow as he grasped another bundle of corn in his left hand, slicing it halfway down the stalk with the sickle. His arms ached and he wondered if he would ever be able to straighten his back again. With gritty determination, the boy kept on harvesting long after his uncle had told him he could stop for the day.

"If I am to take my father's place, then I'll work as long as the other men," he muttered stubbornly.

Finding some shade in the heat of the day, Alexander sat eating his bread and olives alone. He was still sore with his Uncle Calix; dreaming of the time when he would have a home of his own – away from criticism of his father. Perhaps a place his father could return to, one day. Hours later, as daylight started to lose its edge, Alexander felt an arm on his aching shoulder.

"Go home, Alexander, and get some rest. You have worked like a man today. Your father would be proud of you."

Turning his head, Alexander saw his uncle reach out a hand to help him straighten up. It was unusual to hear tenderness in his voice, but Alexander didn't respond to his offer, choosing instead to place the sickle into his uncle's open palm and walk away.

"I miss him too, Alexander," the voice called after him, sadness marking the words.

Alexander walked on in silence, guilt finding its way to his heart because of his bitter attitude. Of course his uncle must miss his father. They were brothers, after all, and once they had been close. Perhaps that's why Uncle Calix always seemed angry with his father – because he loved him and missed him. Perhaps he felt powerless, too.

Dusk covered the town as Alexander made his weary way home, but the town seemed unusually noisy for that time of day. Angry voices could be heard coming from the town square. Alexander was too tired to go and find out what was going on. The words carried on the wind said something about pigs. Somebody had killed some pigs. He wasn't interested.

Reaching home, he had put his hand out to open the door when he heard a familiar voice calling him. It was his long-jumping partner.

"Alexander, did you hear the news?" his friend said, breathlessly.

"If it's about pigs, I don't want to hear," he said abruptly. "I'm too tired."

"But you must listen, Alexander!" his friend continued impatiently, not taking no for an answer. "Some rabbi from across the lake caused two thousand pigs to run into the sea! All the swine from the neighbouring towns have been drowned! The town elders are furious – they've told him to go back where he came from. The pig farmers have lost a fortune!"

"So what?" Alexander said. "I'm too tired to care about pigs!"

"But don't you want to know how he did it, Alexander? No one has ever seen the like before."

"Looks like you're going to tell me, anyway," Alexander yawned.

His friend began to stutter over the words as they spilled out: "The rabbi cast d-d-demons out of a man! And they went into the pigs, and the pigs were so terrorized that they ran down the hill and into the sea! Imagine, Alexander – two thousand pigs! Nearly as many as that legion we saw the other day!"

"Never mind the pigs!" Alexander shouted, his heart now racing with excitement. "What happened to the man?" Without realizing it, he had started to shake his friend by the shoulders, desperate for information concerning the man.

"Who was it? Is he all right? Was this near Gadara? Tell me about the man!" Alexander pleaded.

"OK, OK! Stop shaking me, Alexander!"

"I'm sorry," Alexander replied, stepping back, in an effort to calm himself.

"When the pig owners went back with the swineherds, they found the man sitting calmly at the rabbi's feet. He looked normal again. I mean… he was dressed and… normal. His cuts were all gone, and he was clean. Not screaming, or angry, or anything, but calm and – well – normal!"

"Was it my father?" Alexander pressed his young friend.

"I don't know, Alexander – honestly. I don't know. You know, there have been lots of strange people hanging around the tombs – especially lately."

"Alexander, come in at once!" interrupted his aunt. "This town is no place to be out after dark – not after what happened today."

"But, Aunt… I need to know."

"You'll have to wait until your uncle comes home tomorrow from the threshing floor. He'll find out more then. We have no way of knowing if the man was your father!"

Alexander wasn't the only one who was wondering about the identity of the man who had been delivered from his tormentors by the Jewish rabbi. Catching his arm, his aunt pulled Alexander, protesting, into the house.

In the dimming light of early evening, the man added pace to his stride, realizing he still had a little way to go before reaching home.

Home! The word brought calm to his excited soul. For a long time he had fought to rekindle memories of where that might be. Now, he knew exactly where he was going – Gerasa. He felt a smile stretch across his face as he allowed another memory to lighten his heart. It was the picture of a curly-headed boy – the memory he had struggled to retain during the long months of his time away from home, the time when his life didn't belong to him. Allowing a groan to escape as he remembered the dark, lonely, terrifying ordeal of being possessed by overwhelming forces of evil, the man dismissed the thought with the kind of shout reserved only for victory parades!

He was now free! And the picture of the boy he had tried so hard to identify was now driving him towards home – Alexander, his son.

Thankfully, the city gate was still open, and the man was rather surprised to see people still milling about. With firm determination he set his sights on dwellings just beyond the town square, barely able to contain the joy and excitement that propelled him forwards.

"Is that you, Lysander?" shouted a voice from across the square. "Surely it can't be! I mean, when you left…"

"When I left, I was not myself," Lysander replied, as men started to surround him. "When I left, I was possessed by evil spirits – but today I met with Jesus, the Son of the Most High God."

Those standing around him gasped, realizing that he was the demoniac from whom the demons were cast out. *He* was the man in the "pig story"!

"When I left," he continued, "my name was Legion, 'possessed by many'; but today I return, delivered. You are right; my name is Lysander," he said to the man who had called out to him, "because I am truly the 'one who is freed'." Continuing in the darkness, Lysander told the gathering crowd of how his life had been changed by the one called Jesus. And none could argue, for they could see it with their own eyes.

Alexander pushed his supper around the plate, unable to settle after hearing his friend's story. Outside, he could hear a commotion going on, and it sounded like it was coming closer to his home. A voice that he recognized broke through the sound of many voices.

"Father!"

Rushing to the door, Alexander couldn't believe his eyes. Laughing, crying, jumping up and down, he ran toward the man he had waited for, for so long. Raining kisses on each other, they embraced, their cheeks wet with tears of joy. His father had come home!

And as Alexander looked deep into his eyes, he saw only love looking back at him. He knew this was his real father. The man of his memories – the man of his dreams! Later, as he lay in the crook of his father's arm, he listened to how Jesus had come through the storm to meet with him. Lysander of Gerasa was on the mind of the Son of God – and he came all that way to deliver him, to set him free from his tormentors; to give him control over his life once more. He was no longer powerless!

Then his father spoke of his plans to travel the length and breadth of Decapolis to tell anyone who would listen of all the great things that Jesus had done for him.

With his head resting on his father's chest, Alexander's eyes closed in contented sleep, but not before the boy determined that one day, he too would meet Jesus.

He wouldn't have long to wait.

AD 1979–2005

Mission accomplished! With pockets bulging, Ricky rushed back to where he had hidden his bicycle. Big, dark footprints visibly marked out the shape of the man's boots on the grass, but he knew that the morning sun would soon burn off the dew and with it any evidence he'd ever been there. A victorious whoop escaped from his lips as he swaggered out of the rough on the golf course, the red colours of the dawn peeking over the nearby watery horizon of his coastal home.

Trespassing was a very small misdemeanour in Ricky's eyes; ridding the golf course of a substantial crop of magic mushrooms would, after all, save the greenkeeper a lot of work later in the day, he reasoned. On the other hand, free dope was a real coup for one whose appetite for drugs had become insatiable.

Reaching the road, Ricky stopped under the street light to check the quality of the vegetation now filling his pockets. Even in his drunken stupor he managed to focus on the small tan-capped fungi, gently squeezing one of the long thin stems between his cold fingers. "Yes! It's the real thing," he said, congratulating himself at being able to identify the magic mushroom *psilocybin* by the bluish tinge it produced when under pressure. The memory of the violent sickness that followed his first attempt at harvesting magic mushrooms was not easily forgotten. Ricky learnt quickly that eating just any wild mushroom was a dangerous practice and delivered misery instead of pleasure.

Pleasure… the whole focus of Ricky's existence. As long as he could have fun, it didn't matter how he got it. Life was for enjoying, after all. And he had discovered a long time ago that the consequences of another night of fun were easily diminished by a bottle of Southern Comfort.

The hands on his wristwatch were blurred, and Ricky was surprised at the way the dawn seemed to be following him down the road. Unable to remember what time he had left home the night before, he cycled faster and faster, as he wanted to get a bit of sleep before his favourite day of the week started for real.

Saturday! Saturday was what the rest of the week was all about. Saturday was what Ricky lived for. Saturday was pleasure, spelt with a capital P. Saturday was his and his alone!

The fact that he had been out all night with the punk rock band that he sang with; or that his head was still reeling with the dope they had smoked to boost their raucous bravado; or that he had already consumed his payment for the gig in liquid form was of no consequence. This was only Friday – Saturday was coming!

As the milkman rattled his crates, two doors down from his flat, Ricky looked just like any another drunk trying to do the impossible – put his door key into the lock. With vision blurred and coordination shot, the little piece of metal wouldn't go in the direction its owner wanted it to. Eventually Ricky gave in, banging on the door until he got the required response.

Rebuking him while he was in this state would achieve nothing – she'd seen it too many times before. There was a time when she had joined him in his drinking soirées – then, he had seemed such fun. Now, she was a mother, and responsibility had made her grow up, but not Ricky – he thought he was the Peter Pan of partying, the thirty-something teenager. And so Ricky's partner stood to one side, yet again, and let him head for the bedroom.

"Please, Ricky, don't wake the children," she pleaded, as she watched him stumble upstairs, cursing as he went.

Taking no notice of the request, Ricky opened the door to the children's bedroom, finger pursed to his lips, shushing himself as he sat down on the edge of the bed. Fairy princesses covered the duvet that sheltered the form of a small girl, now stirring with the disturbance in her room.

"Daddy loves you," the slurred words wakening her from her dreams, while his bony fingers slipped gently through her mousey brown curls.

"I love you too, Daddy," came the sleepy reply, her soft little hand patting his cheek.

Yet her words wounded him deeply, the "fun" of the receding night consuming him with guilt as he watched his little girl cuddle her teddy bear to her chest and close her eyes in sleep once more. A solitary tear rolled down Ricky's face, dripping off the end of his chin onto a smiling, pink fabric princess.

You deserve better than me, Princess – what kind of a father am I? I'm nothing but a drunk!

"I thought I asked you not to disturb the children, Ricky!"

"Shut it!" he replied coarsely, angry at the interruption of his thoughts of regret. Wiping his nose on his sleeve before his partner could see the tears, he retorted: "I'll see my children when I want!"

"One of these days, Ricky – one of these days, you'll come

home drunk once too often, and I won't be here when you get back!"

"Don't you threaten me, woman!"

Ricky lifted his hand to strike the mother of his children, but she ran towards the kitchen before the blow could find its target. Sleep was more important now than conflict, so Ricky threw himself on top of his bed, exhausted. Struggling to pull off his good leather jacket, he caught sight of the scars on his wrists; evidence that what made him happy also caused him great pain.

Why, oh why, do I have to feel so miserable after having such a good time? Never mind, it's Saturday – a little sleep, and it'll be party time again!

And as Ricky wrestled with sleep, he had no idea that his life was no longer his own.

"Ricky, can you take the children to the park while I get the shopping in?"

Eyes wide, Ricky stared into the mirror in disbelief.

"Do you know what day it is, woman?"

"Of course I know what day it is, but I need to get to the shops. I won't be long."

"Take them with you. This is *my* day, Saturday, and there's some serious drinking to be done! It's no place for children."

"Every day is your day, Ricky!" she replied, grabbing the children's coats as she lifted her shopping bag.

Hearing the door slammed downstairs, Ricky pushed the tiny pang of regret down even deeper with a pull of the joint he had just lit. It took only seconds to cross the blood–brain barrier, and Ricky quickly began to feel the effects of the substance he needed to set him up for the day ahead; the false courage he required to pretend that he was the coolest guy in town.

His boots were polished to a high shine, while a brass buckled belt held up his best jeans and he slipped his arms into a fine brown leather jacket. A few more drags, to ensure that his courage didn't falter; a reassuring glance at the money in his wallet, and he was ready – for Saturday!

One last look in the mirror and a satisfied smug grin for the man looking back at him: "You're sure to pull tonight," he told the reflection, without a thought for the partner who would be waiting at home for his return.

Holding the shiny handle of the pub door, Ricky breathed deeply, the sense of anticipation bettered only by the buzzing atmosphere that hit him as he walked inside. This was his world, where everyone was your mate; where laughter was heard, banter exchanged and where Ricky felt that he belonged. Around him were mates who emptied their wallets alongside him into the till of the publican – who shared their dope and the stories of how they got it; who'd help to prop him up on his journey home, unless he struck it lucky with some girl out looking for the same end to the night as he was.

It was teatime. The afternoon's sport of cat-calling the referee was now past, the last bet lost. But it was now a different pub, with different drinks, and a big feed of chips helped to mop up the alcohol and give Ricky a boost for what the rest of night promised. Just as his mood started to sink, the phone rang and he sprang out of his seat, hailing the first taxi he saw. Things were looking up – Saturday hadn't failed him, after all.

The thump, thump, thump of the nightclub music was a boost to the ecstasy tablet he had popped into his mouth on the journey down in the taxi. He would show these teenagers a thing or two about clubbing.

He was the world's best dancer, after all… and the world's best liar!

And as he eyed up the talent around the dance floor, he refused to see that his life was not his own, the controlling demons of today rendering him powerless to help himself.

Ricky shivered, as the sun squinted in on him through the bent Venetian blind covering a kitchen window that he didn't recognize. He pulled the old overcoat over his naked shoulders, glancing at pieces of his clothing strewn over someone else's floor.

"Must have been a good night," he muttered, wondering where he was, whom he came home with, and how they got there. The downer side of his ecstasy trip was starting to bite, and he groaned at the thought of what lay ahead. His back was aching, his joints stiff, his flesh shaking, and in the quietness he started to count the tiles, trying to remember.

They were just tiles – nothing special – and there were lots of them. Moving his centre of mathematics to the wall nearest the door, Ricky was startled at the sight before him. Just like Adam and Eve in the Garden of Eden, he squirmed uncomfortably, suddenly aware of his shame and nakedness.

"Who are you, Mister?" said a little voice.

Standing at Ricky's feet was a tousle-headed little boy, with Bob the Builder emblazoned on a pair of grubby pyjamas. Ricky wished for the ground beneath him to swallow him up. But it didn't! This he would have to deal with himself.

"What's ya doing here, Mister?" the young onlooker continued, strawberry jam smeared over his face from the piece of bread in his hand.

Frozen to the spot and with guilt rising like a mountain over him, Ricky felt sickened by this pathetic scene. He had always prided himself in keeping this side of his life from his own children, and now he had been found out by someone else's child. Someone whose name he couldn't even remember. He was speechless.

"Get back to bed with you! What have I told you about coming downstairs before I'm up?"

"But I was hungry!" came the retort, as the little boy ducked away from the slap of the woman who had come to Ricky's rescue. And still Ricky had no idea who she was.

"Hi," he said awkwardly.

"Hello and goodbye, Ricky," she replied, with that look of regret that Ricky had seen on so many "mornings after the night before". Dropping his clothes on top of his chest, she told him to let himself out. Ricky couldn't wait to comply, fleeing homeward; the pictures of the little boy with the jam on his face crowding out any fleeting memories of his fabulous Saturday.

The man looking back at him from the mirror now bore no resemblance to the one he had joked with the day before. Dark rings around his eyes and dried slobber on the side of his mouth made Ricky cringe. It was Sunday… sometime. He didn't know when. He only knew that he felt more guilt, more shame, and more lost than he had done in years.

More lost than when he put up his hand at a gospel-tent campaign, aged eighteen, realizing for the first time that he was a sinner and needed a saviour. More lost than when he had broken up with his Christian girlfriend; more lost than the first time he had attacked another boy on the school bus; or taken his first drink; or drugs.

Somewhere nearby, the church bells rang, their music awakening Ricky's conscience to the guilt and fear that he tried every day to silence with drink and drugs.

"Why is it that I ruin everything I touch?" Ricky shouted into the smoke-filled air. "That's it! I'm through with drink! I mean it, this time!"

Walking to the kitchen, he took the half-empty bottle of spirits, pouring it down the kitchen sink in an effort to mend the tearing of his heart. The fridge was next, cans of beer hissing as the ring-pulls released under Ricky's fingers. Each fizzing drop gurgled down the plughole, without causing any damage to its recipient for once. With a kind of triumphant euphoria, Ricky gathered up the empty cans and bottle, ceremoniously dumping them in the bin. Rubbing his hands in self-satisfied glee, he turned quickly, half expecting to see who it was that had just whispered in his ear.

You've done that before... let's see how long you last this time!

But the mocking words did not come from the room, but from somewhere deep inside, causing Ricky to shake with fear. And it was only then that he noticed how quiet the flat was – no noise from anywhere. In fact, the silence was deafening.

Rushing from room to room, Ricky discovered that he was the only one home. Sunday morning and nobody home?

That can't be.

Wardrobes were half empty; his son's Game Boy gone. His little princess's teddy bear was nowhere to be seen. Sinking into the settee, with his head in his hands, a wailing left Ricky's lips that bounced back off the wall, striking him harder than any of his drunken companions ever had.

"They've gone!" he screamed, kicking the chair across the kitchen.

Anger quickly transformed itself into a despair that rattled around the empty chambers of his broken heart. Guilt beat him up remorselessly as he spent the next hour arguing with himself, one minute blaming his partner for not understanding him, the next blaming himself for his lack of self-control and his poor attempts at fathering.

Standing over the sink, Ricky wished he could suck back all the stuff he had poured down the plughole earlier; but out of the corner of his eye he saw something that would help to blot out his pain for now. And as the magic mushrooms began to transport him to somewhere beyond his heartache, Ricky admitted for the first time that he was… powerless! Powerless to help himself, powerless to turn his life around.

Later, as he was coming down from his trip, lying on a tear-soaked pillow, Ricky slipped into a restless sleep.

With the passing of time, the big yellow truck at the timber yard where Ricky worked became the strangest of companions. He would sometimes envy its ability to lift huge loads of wood with the simple push of a lever. Wood coming from all over the world would pass through his hands, with the burden eventually being lifted by the side-loader. It never seemed to groan under the weight placed on it, and Ricky often wished there was something that could lift *his* burden so easily. But that was only the stuff of dreams, he told himself. Instead, he continued to let his life be controlled by the things that gave him fleeting pleasure; subsequently spending the rest of his time regretting that he had.

Such a vicious cycle of events was taking its toll, and happiness had become harder to find. Years had passed since Ricky had had any contact with church, or even Christians, and he didn't miss it. However, when he wasn't drunk or high, there was a little tugging from deep inside that told him he could be free from the forces that controlled his life. And Ricky knew that was something that he was powerless to do for himself.

One day when the flat was quiet, Ricky blew off the dust from the old Bible that was trapped between his even older school dictionary and a former girlfriend's Mills and Boon novel. His nerves were shot through with trying to keep up the facade of having fun, while he fought the demands of addiction on his life; a fight he always lost.

Even though guilt constantly festered under the surface, Ricky was surprised by what he read in the neglected pages. A big tear splashed on the page where he read the story of the men who were out to punish the adulteress. Jesus had told them that only the one who had never sinned could throw the first stone! The tenderness of Jesus touched Ricky's heart.

Perhaps there is hope for me after all.

Ricky was not aware, at that time, of the promise of God written hundreds of years earlier, saying that "those who seek me and search for me with all their heart shall find me."

But God knew, and as he watched, he saw a man struggle in the darkness, seeking freedom, and for the first time in years Ricky was actually looking in the right direction. Soon Ricky became more familiar with the Bible, and also started to devour Christian books about being set free from the bondage of addictions. But the information itself was not enough to give him the liberty he craved for. And so Saturday remained not only his day, but his dichotomy, because the seeker was still a sinner.

One Saturday evening, Ricky got excited at the possibility of striking it lucky with a woman he had met at the pub. The drink had loosened both of them up, and when she winked, nodding in the direction of the toilets, Ricky followed her. He didn't know how long they had been kissing in the disabled toilet when loud banging and shouting cooled their ardour.

"Get out of there, now!"

The angry screaming made them laugh at first, like silly teenagers, but what followed turned Ricky stone-cold sober in seconds.

"There's a little girl out here sobbing for her mummy! Get out or I'll call the police!"

It wasn't the word "police" that made Ricky's skin crawl, but rather the words "little girl". He hadn't even noticed the woman's daughter; he was too determined to have his way with her mother! And he felt ashamed.

The journey home was like so many before: guilt, remorse and wishing that he could be free – free from the inability to control his life – free from his sin. Stinking with drink and dope, Ricky sat on his sofa, weeping over the life he had lived. Shame and misery had brought him so low that he didn't know where to turn. It all spilled out in a verbal torrent of repentance and a pleading with God whose genuineness found its way to the courts of heaven.

"God, help me! You've got to help me!"

And that night, Ricky's cry was heard.

After so many anguished tears, Ricky was surprised that he had slept. As he lay in the silence, he had no idea what had happened to him. He only knew that he felt different. The constant tossing of his heart had stilled, and yet the stillness didn't frighten him. The flat was empty, but he didn't feel alone. A comforting presence filled every space.

And the church bells rang. And he didn't feel guilty any more. Instead, he felt forgiven… and free!

Jumping out of bed, he ran to the kitchen; down the plughole went the drink once more. Then he surprised himself by destroying the dope and dumping it in the bin! Now, he'd never done that before! And as the day passed into another night's restful sleep, his comfort didn't have to come from a bottle. Ricky's mood was euphoric. He couldn't wait to tell his mates that he was now a new person – a follower of Jesus. Unfortunately, not too many of them were very excited for him; while the men at work took bets on how long it would last – especially as the weekend approached!

But Ricky didn't care. He was experiencing firsthand what Jesus promised in John's Gospel: "When the Son makes you free, you shall be free indeed." He threw himself into studying the Bible, and even turned up at the prayer group of the local church.

Friday night arrived, and the music was blaring. Ricky praised God in the only way he knew how – dancing and jumping around his flat. While the men in his local talked all night about Ricky "getting religion", his seat there remained empty. And hell groaned as Ricky stayed home on Saturday – the victory had been won and another prisoner had been released!

Back at the timber yard, Ricky put the big yellow truck into gear, the words of a song forming in his head – a song, like many others in the days to come, that would bless the lives of people in his community and far beyond. Ricky watched the metal forks lifting a huge load of timber with ease and suddenly recognized that the burden of his sin had been lifted by Jesus, the one who had been nailed to the timber cross so many years ago. The noise of Ricky's singing was drowned out by the drone of the machinery, but he sang all the same.

Your precious blood paid the price I could not pay;
My life of sin, by faith in your blood
Loosed the chains that shackled me
And who am I, that You should know me by my name
And take my shame?
Hallelujah, my God reigns[1]

As the song faded and Ricky stretched to push a lever forward, a recently acquired tattoo became visible on his arm. The words were those of Jesus from the cross; the sentiments, those of an addict, set free for ever!

"It is finished!"

About "Powerless"

c. AD 31

Read for yourself the story of the man known as Legion, as told in Mark's Gospel, chapter 5:1–20.

AD 1979–2005

It is with immense gratitude that I thank Richard "Toadie" Todd for allowing his story to be told in this book. It is not easy to see such a frank account of your life committed to print, but Ricky's deep desire is to see others avoid the addictions that rendered him powerless for so long.

A talented singer-songwriter, Ricky continues to bless and

1. "Precious Blood" from the album Wedding by Richard Toadie Todd, Upstream Recordings.

challenge young and old alike through his music and testimony. His life reinforces the message that true freedom is to be found in Jesus Christ.

Important biblical references in Ricky's story:

John 8:3–11, Jeremiah 29:13, John 8:36, John 19:30.

Loveless

C. 2085 BC

Perhaps this would be an end to it!

The ivory comb slid through the strands of silky hair with such ease. No tangles, no knots; just elegant, long, flowing dark locks crowning a head of such beauty as the handmaid had rarely seen before. Both women maintained an uncomfortable silence. The girl's mistress knew she was now the root of all the gossip circulating in the palace harem. Accusing looks from behind pillars accompanied whispering and even bold, smirking laughter, all directed at the foreign princess, Pharaoh's recent acquisition.

Now the air was electrified with the latest revelations!

The young servant felt a surge of pity for her mistress as she continued her morning beauty programme, knowing only too well that perfumes and creams couldn't smooth away the hurt and disappointment she must be feeling.

"But surely this would be an end to all the sickness now?" she repeated in the quiet places of her mind, still somewhat unconvinced that the circulating rumours could be true.

As she had rushed from her sleeping quarters earlier that morning, before dawn had broken, she was stopped by a friend who was on her way to the palace kitchen.

"What do you think of your mistress now, Hagar? She'll be lucky if she keeps that lovely head of hers! I wouldn't like to be in her shoes for all the sand in Egypt!"

"What silly nonsense are you talking about now?" Hagar replied, squeezing her brow into a frown, while straightening her pleated skirt as she walked.

"Didn't you hear?" her friend continued, trying to get Hagar to pay attention as they quickly traversed the marble-lined corridors. "Once he saw that Pharaoh liked how his wife looked, that husband of hers told the palace officials that she was his sister – just to save his own skin! Imagine that! He even accepted a huge bride price for her – sheep, oxen, donkeys, camels and slaves! How would you like a husband like that, eh?"

"I don't believe you; you're making it up! You'll have to stop all this gossiping. It's going to get you into trouble some day."

"Honestly, Hagar, it *is* true this time!" her friend protested, as she turned down the stairwell leading to the kitchens. "And if she goes, you'll be back in the kitchen with me in no time – mark my words!"

Hagar arrived in the harem flustered at the news she had just heard, trying to dismiss it as mere gossip, of the sort regularly passed on by her friend.

Now, a few hours later, with comb in hand, she knew from more reliable sources that it was all true. Her mistress, a princess from the magnificent city of Ur, had indeed been given by her merchant-prince husband into the harem of the Pharaoh. Some were even saying that her god was raining down judgment on them because of it. In fact, if it hadn't been for the sickness plaguing the palace since her arrival, she would surely have been in the bedroom of the Pharaoh by now. A sigh unwittingly escaped from Hagar's lips as her fingers sectioned off the dark tresses, causing her mistress to look up.

"Hagar!"

The girl stiffened.

"Hagar, no partitions today. Fix my hair as it was when I arrived: a long plait, twisted and pinned around my head. I am no longer to be an Egyptian queen, but to be returned to my husband. I am going home."

Hagar noticed a slight quiver in her mistress's lower lip, while a solitary tear slipped down over her perfectly sculptured cheekbone. She may have been a proud woman, but Hagar sensed that the tears were those of relief rather than disappointment, and the girl wondered how she could possibly be happy to return to a man who had given her up so easily. That was something she would know soon enough.

The rest of the morning was spent packing. Hagar busily folded beautiful silks and woollen throws, somewhat surprised that her mistress was allowed to take it all with her. It appeared that Pharaoh feared further trouble from this god of hers, and so everything she had touched was to go with her – including Hagar!

Hagar's life had not been her own since the day her father sold her into service at the palace, but she had never dreamt then that she would belong to anyone but Pharaoh. A mix of intense emotions filled the young woman's heart as she walked several steps behind her new mistress to meet the man who had caused all the trouble leading to this day, and to start out on her new life. What lay ahead, Hagar had no idea.

The palace guard surrounded the man Hagar assumed was the merchant prince, husband of her mistress. *He was indeed lucky to have kept his life! I wouldn't have been so kind!* But Hagar knew she must keep her thoughts to herself, as her mistress bowed deferentially to the man she heard addressed as Abram. But what was the look she saw passing between them in that moment of reserved, respectful reunion? As their eyes met, Hagar saw something she had never witnessed in the palace harem – a look of affection. *She loved him!* Hagar couldn't believe it, and yet a slight tinge of jealousy entered her heart, for although her mistress had been wronged, she was also loved; something that Hagar had never experienced in her life.

She was a slave to her circumstances; no one would ever love her.

"Collecting water isn't my job!" Hagar protested. "I'm here to look after my mistress, not to walk to the well!"

"Listen here, my girl, you're not in Pharaoh's palace now!" came the stern reply from the manager of Abram's household. "You'll go to the well with the rest of the women, or there will be no bath for your mistress! What will she say to that?"

Hagar grunted sarcastically as she lifted an earthen pot onto her head. "Bath! There's never enough water out here in the middle of nowhere for a bath!" she muttered. "Why didn't she stay in the luxury of Egypt? Then I could have prepared a 'sea' of perfumed oil for her, instead of the basin she has to make do with in this wilderness!"

As she made the journey to the well, Hagar reminisced on all she had been taken away from. Gone were solid buildings with stone floors and marble-lined rooms filled with beautiful things. Gone was the security of living in the safest place in Egypt. Gone was the comfort of the familiar. Gone was her friend, who filled her head with the wildest of stories. How she missed them all!

In their place were tents – more tents than she could count! Long, flat dwellings made of woven goat's hair, attached to poles and pitched on grass! No permanency, no stone floors, no elegant marble, no golden statues; children and animals free to roam anywhere they wished. Oh yes, the inside of her tent was decorated with silks and beautifully woven mats that had been bought in lands she had only heard of before. Heavily embroidered curtains did section off the private rooms of Abram and her mistress, Sarai, while she slept on a rolled-out mat in a little corner of the tent. As she cast her eyes over the tent city stretched out before her, Hagar recognized that Abram must be wealthy to own all this; but it still wasn't home.

"How is it that so many people come to be wandering from place to place, far away from anywhere?" she dared to ask another servant girl as they walked back from the well, jars safely balancing on their heads.

"Don't you know?" came the surprised reply. "Abram was told by God to leave his country and to go to another land that God would show him."

"And which god was that?" interrupted Hagar.

"Don't let Abram hear you talk like that!" the girl scolded, as if Hagar should know better. "Why, it was the Lord God who told him – the 'one, true God'. And do you know what else God told Abram?"

"No; but I think you are going to tell me," she added, smirking at the ridiculous idea of only *one* god.

"God told Abram that he would make him to be the father of a great nation one day!"

"Funny, that," replied Hagar, "when he doesn't even have any children." Taking her new-found friend by the arm, Hagar continued, "I think we're going to get on well – you remind me of a friend I left back in Egypt. She used to tell me wild fanciful stories too."

"But it is true – honestly!"

"Yes, yes," Hagar sighed knowingly. She had heard enough for now.

Time passed quickly in her constantly moving home. The chores were unending. Grain had to be ground into flour; cheese made from goats' milk; cloth woven from hand-spun wool; and stews made for the evening meals. Stews – ah, Hagar often wished that she had some of those wonderful leeks and garlic from Egypt to spice up the bland pots of stew they made in Canaan! Her twice-daily trek to the well with her new friend became a break from her mistress; a time when she could be herself and talk about what she wanted to talk about. It was during these times that her friend filled her in with all the local gossip, as well as continuing her education about these Sumerian people that she lived among – especially Abram and Sarai.

Then, just when you were getting used to a new location, down came the tents and off you would go again. Hagar hated these times of striking camp. Her mistress Sarai was usually tetchy when so much had to be done, watching Hagar's every move – and you could be sure that if something was broken, Hagar got the blame! But the transit of such a huge crowd was something to behold. Over a thousand people, with herds of sheep, goats and camels; and what a noise they made, as they left barren pastureland and bare bushes in their wake.

With so many people to please, things were difficult at times, and Hagar saw Abram's wisdom brought to bear on many occasions, especially with regard to his nephew Lot. The herdsmen fought more regularly than the animals! Eventually the huge company was divided in two, as Lot headed off towards the fertile Jordan valley with its lush grazing land, while Abram stayed in Canaan, moving to Mamre, at Hebron.

Peace and friendly relations were resumed and the sound of children playing rang through the air around the camp once more.

Children. Hagar loved to watch them play, but any time they came near to Abram's tent she could see her mistress's smile disappear and her eyes mist over. For Sarai had no children, and her heart was broken with the shame she felt. Not to give your husband sons was to fail as a wife – never mind the ache of empty arms that she felt herself. Hagar's young friend had told her that this "one, true God" had promised Abram children twelve years earlier, when he had left Haran at God's command. It didn't make much sense to Hagar, as Abram still had no children!

Maybe they should try to plead with some other gods to give them children! Hagar thought one day, as she heard the regular anguished cry of her mistress coming from deep inside the tent. *Surely Nanna, the moon god of Ur, would grant them fertility, or even Hathor, the Egyptian goddess of love.*

But there were no shrines in the tents of Abram; no golden idols, no stone statues, no figures of wood. Hagar had only ever seen her master build one altar, and that was at Bethel. There she watched him call on the name of the Lord, the one he said had appeared to him there before. But Hagar didn't see any god.

Anyway, what god would be interested in a slave? Still, she sighed as she watched Sarai's sadness deepen with her increasing years, any chance of motherhood fading with each passing day. Why Abram still believed that this "god" would keep his promise and make him a father of a great nation was a mystery to Hagar.

It's hard to keep secrets in a tent; and on this particular day Hagar couldn't believe what she was hearing! Something was going on and, somehow or other, Hagar knew that she was part of the plot.

Sarai was speaking in hushed tones, as Hagar tiptoed towards the curtain in an effort to hear what was going on. "The Lord has prevented me from having children, Abram. I want you to take my maid Hagar as your 'wife' – maybe she will have children for me. Perhaps God's promise will be given through her."

Hagar stepped back in shock, covering her mouth quickly to stifle a gasp. Heated words ensued, but Hagar didn't hear any more, as she tried to process what her mistress had just said. Her heart was racing; she felt sick. She was to be given to Abram, but she knew she would only be a "wife" to him in his bed. Abram loved Sarai. Hagar belonged to Sarai. Sarai could do what she wanted with her. It was a simple transaction – a means to an end. Hagar was to be used – but she would not be loved.

Before long, a little tent was erected beside Abram's tent. Hagar would have her own home, yet still belong to Sarai. Sometimes, she even dared to dream that perhaps, if she tried hard enough, Abram might love her as he loved Sarai. But the dream always disappeared as quickly as morning mist in the presence of the sun's early rays. Her nights were restless, as she kept her eavesdropping to herself, even her friend remarking on her quiet mood as they walked together to the well.

Hagar wasn't the only one who had little to say.

Abram seemed distant, his thoughts preoccupied. The atmosphere between the merchant prince and his princess was more strained than Hagar had ever witnessed before. Then it happened.

Hagar discovered that she hadn't imagined the conversation after all. One morning, in a manner as matter-of-fact as when she instructed Hagar on what to prepare for breakfast, Sarai told Hagar: "I have given my husband permission to go into your tent tonight. You are to be his 'wife' according to our custom, and perhaps he will have a son through you, my maid."

"Yes, Mistress," were the only words Hagar could squeeze from her trembling lips.

In the servant world, Hagar's position as personal maid to someone of Sarai's prominence was one to be envied. But today the young Egyptian didn't feel privileged. Rather, she realized that she was just another of her mistress' possessions, to be used as her owner wished. And so Hagar prepared for what lay ahead; only the perfumed oils didn't seem to smell as sweet any more.

Next morning, as the dawn peeked between the gaps in her tent, Hagar stretched her arm out over the empty space beside her. It was cold. Abram had left in the night, as soon as his "task" had been completed. In their brief moments of embrace, something stirred in Hagar that she had always tried to bury in the deep recesses of her heart. Something that as a slave she had tried to protect herself from – the need for companionship, belonging and love.

But the gnawing hole where these emotions were meant to reside gapped wider than ever on that particular morning, as her silk pillow swallowed up her tears. Hagar was loveless.

Some weeks later, Hagar couldn't understand why the smell of the bread baking in her clay oven was causing her tummy to do somersaults. For days now she had been feeling queasy and dreaded her cooking chores, having almost fainted the previous evening as she ladled out the spicy bean stew. But for Abram's steadying hand, she felt sure she would have fallen into the fire.

"And you honestly can't work out what's wrong with you, Hagar?" her friend asked, with a look of disbelief.

"No," Hagar groaned. "I just feel sick all the time."

"You're pregnant, you silly girl!" her friend announced, with a wry grin. "What's Sarai going to say about that, eh?"

"She'll be delighted, I guess; it's just what she wanted."

"No!" her friend gasped. "I don't believe you. Abram! No – you poor thing! Why didn't you tell me?"

"Didn't want to – it's all legal and above board, you know," Hagar continued, trying to convince herself as much as her friend. "According to their law, Sarai is allowed to give her maid to her husband, if she can't have any children of her own."

"But still – Abram! I thought..." Her words tailed off as she looked at her friend's sad face; linking Hagar's arm in her own, she tried to lighten her burden: "Imagine, Hagar, a baby of your own – how exciting!"

And a tiny spark of delight surged in Hagar's heart.

Abram and Sarai's pleasure was more subdued. Their scheming may have been successful, but they knew they had not waited for the promise of God. Both were inwardly aware that their meddling with God's will was a sign of unbelief. *But Abram was going to have a child. Surely that was all that mattered?* Or so Sarai thought. Meanwhile, Hagar blossomed.

By the time the sheep would lamb in the spring, she would have offspring of her own. It was a thought that kept a constant smile on her face. Yet, with the smile, a smirk grew. Hagar's feeling of resentment towards Sarai was such that she now became bold in her speech with her mistress, chiding her that she couldn't give Abram an heir while she, a mere servant, would give her master the child he so desired.

Hagar's constant arrogance compounded the feeling of failure that Sarai was trying to hide, while the maid's enlarging abdomen added insult to the injury of childlessness she had experienced every day of her adult life. Eventually, Sarai could take it no longer. In the mother of all rows, Sarai fought with Abram, abused Hagar and compounded the misery of that unhappy home.

Life couldn't get any worse! Hagar knew that Abram didn't love her, that her mistress hated her and that the child she was carrying would never be accepted in their home. Nursing her bruised body and aching heart, she headed for the well with her friend and kept on walking – far away from the tents of Abram – far away from the angry, bitter Sarai. And in her heart, home called to her. So she kept on walking.

She had no idea what she was going to tell her father when she arrived home; she only hoped that perhaps he would be able to do what he hadn't been able to before – love her.

The road back to Egypt was long – and very lonely. Hagar rested in the heat of the day, stroking her swollen tummy, speaking to the child she carried in the security of her body. His strong kicks were the only communication she had with anyone, on the desert road to Shur. Until, that is, she stopped to drink at a spring of water near to the border with Egypt.

A palm tree provided some shade, as Hagar tried to stay away from the merchant traders who had stopped to water their camels on their long journey. She knew only too well that a woman travelling alone was unwise and unsafe, but her determination had not wavered until she heard a voice call her name.

"Hagar, Sarai's maid."

Hagar gasped, pushing her body firmly against the prickly

bark of the tree, her eyes darting from side to side, scanning the surrounding countryside. *Who could possibly know my name out here in this wilderness?* Glancing down the road, she saw the last of the camel caravans rounding the bend in the dusty road. For the first time in hours, the spring was deserted by man or beast. Fear almost took her breath away. *Who could know that I am Sarai's maid? Perhaps the sun is playing tricks on me. Perhaps Abram has sent someone after me?*

The voice continued; not harsh, as so many voices had been to her in the past. Instead, an unusual gentleness washed over her.

"Where have you come from, and where are you going to?" the voice asked; but Hagar had a suspicion that the enquirer already knew the answer. Somehow or other, he was giving her the opportunity to own up to what she had done.

Then she saw him. The brightness of the sun behind him made it difficult for Hagar to make out his features. Yet she felt that she should know him. He wasn't like anyone she had encountered before – certainly like no other man she had ever met. His manner was authoritative, yet considerate. She wasn't afraid of this stranger. And she felt compelled to answer him truthfully: there didn't seem any point in hiding anything from him.

"I'm running away," she said firmly, "running away from my mistress, Sarai."

Then the man, who knew Hagar's name, continued to speak with the sad, lonely runaway. He seemed to know everything about her: not only her past, but her future as well. After telling her to return to her mistress, he told Hagar about the child she carried; the family that would one day become a nation that could not be numbered.

She wept when the man said: "You will have a son; you shall call his name Ishmael." And she wept with joy at the knowledge that she would have a son to love and care for; wept at the realization that he would not be a slave but a free man, strong and without fear; wept at the name given to him.

"Ishmael – because the Lord has heard your affliction."

The Lord has heard my *affliction!* Hagar couldn't believe it! *The God of heaven saw* my *pain – the anguish of a mere slave – and he sent his angel to tell me!* Yes! At last Hagar saw the truth of what was unfolding before her eyes. This was no mere man. The "one, true God", whom her friend had told her about, really was a living God, and he had sent his angel directly to tell her that everything was going to be all right. No – it was more than that. God had sent his angel to assure Hagar that her name was known in heaven; her pain was felt in heaven; and her future security would come from heaven. And something rose from that secret place that Hagar had spent a lifetime trying to ignore, never believing that she would ever experience its presence for herself.

It was the indescribable feeling of being loved. Loved!

And she knew at that moment that in spite of her circumstances; in spite of the fact that she might never know human love; God would take care of her and her son. That God loved the slave girl from the land of Egypt so much that he had sent his angel to tell her personally.

Or… had he actually come himself?

The thought overwhelmed her, as she watched him turn

away and leave her alone. Alone – no! Hagar knew she would never be alone again. She had met with El Roi, the "Living One, who sees me!" And felt his love.

AD 1970–2002

"Just you wait til your da comes home!"

Donna stiffened as the sharp smack caught the nape of her neck. She had tried so hard all week to do everything that her mother had asked. Now the broken cup lying at the eight-year-old's feet was all that was needed for her to dread her father's return at the end of the week. Barely feeling the little cut in her finger from the broken crockery, Donna tried not to dwell on the beating that was to come. It was only Wednesday, after all. Friday was two days away, and she knew that there was no way she'd have been able to please her mother for all that time, anyway.

Maybe her father would come home in a good mood this weekend, she thought to herself whilst brushing the results of her clumsiness onto a piece of old cardboard. Heading for the bin, Donna couldn't stop the picture of her father's big broad leather belt from forming in her mind. A weary sigh slipped from her mouth. She never seemed to be able to do anything right, or to be able to come up with any way to make her mother love her.

I'm just a bad girl. That's what everybody says about me. It must be true.

Donna's thoughts were interrupted by the harsh call of

the one she had grown to fear. She knew immediately what the problem was. The baby was crying, and it was her job to make sure that he didn't!

"Donna! You lazy good-for-nothing! Do you not hear that baby?"

Before her mother could reach her with another slap, Donna had lifted her little baby brother out of the rough home-made crib beside the fire, shushing him for all she was worth.

"I'll take him out in the pram, Ma," she said, heading for the hallway of their overcrowded flat. "Maybe the rocking will put him back to sleep."

"That'll do," was the reply. "But make sure you're back here to help with the tea. I can't be expected to do everything around here!"

Pulling on her coat in readiness for the cold Dublin air, Donna headed outside, hoping that a little walk around the block would calm her fretful little brother. It was hard being the big girl in the family. Sometimes she wished that her mother's first daughter was still alive, because then maybe Donna would have some help in looking after her other three brothers and one sister. But she wasn't alive, and so Donna resigned herself to her lot in life. After all, you are a big girl when you're eight. That's what her mother had told her.

But then, Donna never remembered being a little girl.

Leaning over the balcony of the run-down block of flats that was home, Donna called one of the teenage lads from the street below to help her lift the pram down the stone steps. Her baby brother was a cute little thing, and Dublin folk are like others the world over: they love to admire babies! Soon Donna had an audience of adoring neighbours tickling the baby's chin and making all kinds of cooing noises at him.

"You're a good girl, Donna, helping your ma the way you do," said a woman from across the street, smiling as she did so.

Donna warmed with the compliment, returning the smile. It was a rare thing to be praised, and the little girl felt a foot taller as she walked on with the pram. Donna hadn't noticed what time it was when she left home, but as she passed the school, a short distance from where she lived, she heard the finishing bell ring. Darting down a side street, Donna put some distance between her and the school gate. She'd be in trouble if the nuns saw her, as she'd missed yet another day at school, on her mother's insistence to stay at home and help.

"I'm never going to learn my times tables if Ma keeps me home any longer," she told her little brother, who was smiling at the bouncing action of the pram as they made their getaway.

Once his little eyes began to droop, Donna headed for home, hoping that getting him up the stairs wouldn't undo her efforts.

Maybe if Ma got a little house over the river, instead of living here, she'd be happier, Donna thought as she struggled to mount the steps. Before she even opened the door, Donna heard her younger sister getting an earful from her mother, so she left the sleeping infant in the pram outside the door on the balcony. There was bread to be buttered, and three other hungry mouths waiting for her return.

She was right. Donna found catching up on the times tables very difficult after missing so much school, and the nuns had no sympathy with her plight. They were there to educate the children of inner-city Dublin and had no time for slackers. Sitting in the dunces' corner the next day, Donna tried very hard to learn the lessons she had missed since her little brother had been born. Her knuckles were stinging from the smack of the wooden ruler that the teacher called her "attention grabber", but Donna had learned outside the classroom to keep her eyes dry and her tears to herself. With a face set like flint, devoid of emotion, the little eight-year-old stared at the numbers in front of her, reciting them silently in her head. She hoped against hope that when asked to say them out loud, she would get it right and avoid the laughter of her peers, which was worse than the pain of the ruler.

You are useless! Just like your ma says.

Try as she might, Donna couldn't stop the lone tear that escaped down her face, dropping on the page below. It was Thursday. Friday was coming.

The following afternoon, the sound of the school finishing bell made Donna jump. She put her exercise book into her schoolbag and headed for the door, lifting her coat from its peg as she passed by. Her footsteps dragged, as she made her way slowly through the playground. Her chin seemed stuck against her chest as she glumly passed some classmates, who were excitedly running around looking forward to the weekend break. To add insult to injury, she watched as one little girl ran into the arms of her father, waiting for her at the school gate. He twirled her around in the air and planted a big kiss on her cheek before setting her back on the ground.

Donna knew her father would be waiting for her, too – but not with a kiss.

Maybe Ma will have forgotten to tell him about the broken cup.

She hadn't.

"Am I ever going to come home to find that you have managed to see a week through without getting into trouble?" were the words that greeted her as she tried to sneak down the hallway.

There was no point in answering. Donna simply stiffened as the leather belt whipped around her bare legs, causing her to lose her balance. Curled into a ball on the floor, she protected her pale face as the beating continued, the pain searing through her skinny body. The baby cried, but Donna remained silent. Her siblings scattered, but Donna remained still.

"Look what you've made me do!" cried the man standing over her, his face still carrying the grime of his week's work. "If you would do what you are told, this wouldn't have to happen. It's your own fault!"

Donna said nothing; the hatred she felt for her father was exceeded only by her hatred for her mother.

Why can't they love me? Even just a little.

Because you are a bad girl, Donna… just like the auld fella says.

The words in her head were easier to believe with each passing Friday, and Donna was sure that no one would ever love her. Becoming tough was the only way to survive.

Developing a thick skin was achievable in her waking

hours; but she had no protection from what happened in her sleep. Dreams tormented the hours that were meant to bring her rest. One dream in particular disturbed the child over and over again, its contents so dark that Donna didn't dare share them with a living soul. It made her feel dirty, and yet she didn't know why. Try as she might, the dream could only be remembered in parts. Donna feared that the hidden parts might be her fault, and for that reason she kept the torture to herself.

"Billy the liar! Billy the liar!" chanted the child in her dream.

Donna recognized the child as herself, very young, perhaps around three years of age. One minute she is skipping to her grandmother's house with a two-shilling coin in her hand; the next she's at the Bridewell police station with her mother. The policemen seem nice, and they aren't cross with her. They are all in a small room, and a doctor is examining her. When he is finished, her mother is very angry and drags Donna home. The auld fella is waiting for them, and there is a lot of shouting. On this occasion he isn't cross with her, but Donna knows something must have happened – she just can't remember what. But it must be her fault, so she decides not to ask her mother or anyone else.

At ten years of age, Donna was becoming street-savvy. Life was hard, and not only for her family. Crammed into the streets around where she lived were large family groups, crowded into poor housing. High levels of unemployment meant money was scarce, and people used what they could to attempt an escape from their problems. Smoking and drinking alcohol were often more important than eating. Donna soon started picking up discarded cigarette ends from the streets. By the time she was fourteen, her mother gave her ten cigarettes a day. It was easier than making her lunch. Smoking made Donna feel like the big girl everyone told her she was.

When Donna arrived home from school one day, a new member had been added to the family. A boy of eleven, he was a year older than Donna: short, smelly and fat, and starting to get spots. Donna's ma was all over him with affection, and Donna soon heard how his own mother had thrown him out on the streets. Now, out of the kindness of her heart, Donna's ma announced that he would live with them from now on!

"Where will he sleep, Ma?" Donna asked, picturing their already crowded bedroom.

"There's plenty of room," her mother replied. "He can share the bed with the young 'un."

And so number six was added to the family – the first child in the house to be treated with any display of affection from her mother. It seemed that this boy could do no wrong.

Saturday nights were drinking nights in the family, and Donna dreaded them. Toleration went out of the window when drink was consumed, and fighting was sure to follow. Donna tried to ensure that she and the younger children were in bed before her parents returned from the pub. The bedroom was small. Donna and her sister shared one set of bunk beds, while two of her brothers shared the bunks opposite. The new arrival slept in the remaining single bed with her little brother. If Donna reached out, she could touch all the beds without stretching.

One Saturday night, Donna woke with a fright. Someone was in her bed! She knew instantly that it wasn't one of the little ones, looking for a cuddle after a bad dream. She could feel little fat fingers running over her body, touching her in places that were meant for her alone! Her heart was beating faster. She was afraid to breathe; afraid to call out! A voice whispered threats of what would happen if she screamed – or if she told. He threatened to tell her ma that she had asked him to do it; in fact, begged him.

"And you know how much your ma likes me!" he teased. "She'll never believe you!"

Donna knew that he was right. This "adopted" brother of hers could do no wrong in her mother's eyes; she would believe him over her own daughter any day. So the lovely ten-year-old became sullied in her own bed, longing for her father's belt, rather than the pain that was now being inflicted on her. It was a filthy blow to her childhood innocence; another dark secret to lock away with the mounting pain in her life.

Donna lay in silence as he played with her body, quivering and unable to move, for fear of worse. When he slipped out of her bed, Donna knew he would be back. She was his new toy. And no one must ever know!

Saturdays were no better than Fridays.

Time passed, but nothing ever changed for Donna. Now at secondary school, Donna learnt more than reading and writing. She wasn't the only one to suffer abuse in her own home. One day she heard some girls talking about running away; as she listened, she put her own plan into action.

The "great escape" happened one morning when, instead of going to school, Donna headed in the opposite direction. It was a dark, miserable morning as the twelve-year-old made her way across the Halfpenny Bridge, but it wasn't as dark and miserable as she felt inside. She couldn't take it any longer. Maybe if she didn't come home, her ma and da would realize how unhappy she was, and maybe they would throw the brute out on the streets for what he was doing to her. People on their way to work jostled the young girl as they passed her on the narrow footbridge; strangers, who had no idea of the drastic measures this young girl was taking in her bid to escape from her miserable life.

Donna almost lost her nerve, as she walked down the street that straddled the chapel. At the back of the church building stood the convent, her place of refuge. As Donna put her finger on the bell of the big oak door, she almost hoped that no one would answer. Her bravery was starting to wane when the door suddenly opened, making her step back in fright. The nun standing in front of her in full black habit recognized her fear and spoke softly.

"Yes, what can I do for you?" was all she said.

"Can I come in?" Donna replied, visibly shaking.

"Are you in trouble?" asked the nun, who looked kindly at the distraught child.

"Yes," was the only reply that Donna could manage.

The warm sweet tea brought more than relief to a grumbling tummy. Donna felt safe; yet as the day wore on, she knew that her ma would be wondering where she was, and fear took over once more.

The nun tried to get Donna to tell her why she had come, but Donna's replies were vague. It was clear that the child was unhappy at home, but they needed more than that to allow a child to stay away from her family. The secrets of her heart stayed right where they were. Donna was never going to tell anyone. They would have to find them out for themselves.

Social services personnel did no better; and when they returned from Donna's home, having been thrown out by her father, their understanding had turned to anger. If she wouldn't tell them what had happened to her, then they couldn't help her. So Donna was sent back home.

The few days at the convent had been like heaven. What she went home to wasn't. As soon as the social worker left the flat, the frenzied beating began. Donna wanted to shout out – maybe the social worker would hear her and come back to rescue her. Donna's head felt like it was on fire, as her father dragged her across the room by the hair. She heard an almighty crack as he threw her against the wall. Darkness enveloped the child, as the first blow of his broad leather strap came across her back. Maybe she would die.

That would be nice.

When Donna arrived home from hospital later that day, she nursed a head injury but she was still alive. From there on in, she knew that if she was going to survive she would have to become tough. No one loved her, and she didn't love anyone either. In this loveless world that she lived in, it was all about survival. And she was going to survive.

For the next few years, Donna stayed out of the house as

much as she could. Drink and cigarettes helped to numb the pain and to get her through each day. She mixed with a rough crowd and always met boys who promised her the earth if she would go with them. Deep inside, she had a dream that perhaps one day someone would mean what they said and really love her.

One young man in particular tugged at her heart. He was handsome, and promised her that he would look after her and not let anybody hurt her again. Donna was fourteen when she ran away with him to his flat in North Dublin. They started their great adventure with cider and a tablet of some kind. When she woke in the morning the bed was covered in blood. Donna had no memory of what he had done to her. But she liked him, and stayed for a week before deciding that he was just like all the rest and headed back home.

The belt was waiting, but it didn't matter any more. Donna was past caring what anyone did to her. Home would do, until she was old enough to have one of her own.

Four months later, Donna lay in Dublin's maternity hospital. Still only fourteen, her heart was filled with mixed emotions. Excitement had grabbed her when the doctor told her she was pregnant. She gasped at the thought of having someone of her own to love, a warm glow coming from a place she didn't know she possessed. In those brief seconds she pictured herself holding a little baby in her arms. But the doctor was still speaking to her mother as she was daydreaming, and his words felt like the slap of a cold flannel.

"I'm afraid it is unlikely that this baby will survive."

"That's good," her mother replied. "She's far too young to have a baby, and I can't look after another one!"

The cutting remark broke Donna's heart.

The next few days brought about what the doctor had said was inevitable. Donna soon convinced herself that it was just as well, especially following the visit of an aunt who told her in no uncertain terms what kind of a girl she was. The scene in the ward was violent and embarrassing, except for the kindness of a fellow patient, who showed Donna that maybe there are people who could understand her pain.

It was almost Christmas when Donna made her sad, weary way home from hospital. The lights of the tree looked almost welcoming, but Donna knew better than to believe that it meant anything for her.

Her father waited until the New Year before he doled out the punishment his daughter "deserved" for bringing such a disgrace on the family. He didn't want to spoil Christmas for the rest of the family, or so he had said. Donna welcomed another year with stab wounds to her chest and broken ribs. And she hated him.

The next few years passed much the same as the others. Sometimes Donna would work at a local clothing factory and sometimes she would go to school. Then she would run away again, but always return for another beating. And every time she ran away she felt guilty, because she knew that her "adopted" brother climbed into her younger sister's bed while she was away.

And she hated herself nearly as much as she hated the boy who had become the "apple of her mother's eye".

"It's your own fault!" the voice in her head would say in her quiet moments. And she believed it.

When she was sixteen, Donna left home for good. She never loved anybody, and she always came to regret her choice in men. Not one of them appeared to have the capacity to love her. But then, Donna didn't know how to love, either. It was only the stuff of films and books. It never happened to real people like her. Getting safely through the day was about the best you could hope for.

By the time she was a woman, she had learnt to fight her corner. She could give as good as she got. Violence was a way of life. A way to protect yourself. A way to stay alive.

When she was twenty-two she moved in with the man who was to become her long-term partner. Love didn't come easy; he was just there, and Donna was tired of moving about. Already with one child by a previous partner, Donna stayed put. But their relationship was extremely volatile.

He was just like her father – in so many ways. Beatings and abuse had become a way of life for the pretty, brown-haired young woman. And when she was drunk she fought back; but she wasn't strong enough to inflict as much damage on him as he did on her.

And, after all these years, the dream continued to torment her sleeping hours. Even as an adult, she had no idea what it meant.

When the children came along, Donna cared for them to the best of her ability. She wanted her own children to know what it was to be hugged; to be touched in ways other than those of violence. It was hard. They frequently witnessed fierce rows, violent outbursts and the abuse of their mother. She had four sons of her own, as well as caring for her sister's son, before she finally had a little girl.

"Ma, can I go to the club?" one of the boys asked one day.

"What club, Son?"

"The one in Chancery Place, Ma. Me mate says it's great fun. They've got a snooker table, and you get free juice and biscuits. And they tell you stories. Can I go, Ma, please?"

"OK, but be back before it gets dark – do ya hear me?"

The sound of the door slamming was the only reply that Donna got. Before long, each of the boys headed out on various days to the club. They loved it. Soon Donna heard about the stories that followed the games sessions. They were stories about Jesus, so she couldn't complain about that. What mattered was that it kept her children off the street and out of the house when things were bad between her and her partner. The people at the club even helped with the children's homework, much to Donna's delight.

Asking around, Donna discovered that the clubs were run by Christians who were different from most church folk. They didn't look down on families like hers because they were poor, and they really seemed to care about the kids in the neighbourhood. Donna was glad, because by now her life was at its lowest ebb.

She was now thirty-five and still held so many dark secrets deep inside: things that she had never told another soul – like her dream. Then, one day, a cousin innocently asked if she had ever heard what had happened to "Billy, the liar". Donna nearly collapsed at the shock of hearing someone talk about her dream.

"How do you know about my dream?" she shouted, frightening her cousin with her angry response.

"What dream? I don't know about your dream. I was just talking about the old man who assaulted you, when you were only three!"

Donna sank back into her chair. The dream was not what it had seemed all these years. The torture of her sleep was a memory, not a dream. No one had ever told her. No one had ever thought of talking to her about the day the old man gave her money for "hurting" her. And no one ever loved her enough to make sure she had recovered from the ordeal.

That was probably my fault too, she thought, *just like ma always said it was*. Like the day her mother found out about what had happened in Donna's bed for all those years. Just as she expected, in her ma's eyes it was Donna's fault, and she smashed an ornament into her daughter's face for daring to suggest otherwise. And all of it brought a darkness into Donna's soul.

Then one afternoon Donna opened her front door to find a smiling face looking straight at her. The young woman spoke with an American twang, but Donna soon found out that it was a Canadian accent, not American.

"I'm from the club," she said, "just thought I'd come by and say hello."

That was the beginning of a deep friendship that was spoiled by only one thing. Her visitor kept asking Donna to go to church with her, and Donna kept making excuses, one of which was, in fact, valid. Donna had agoraphobia. She rarely ever went out, the past having caught up with her mental state. However, her new-found friend persisted, constantly telling Donna that she was praying for her. That was something Donna was grateful for, but not hopeful of. After all, why would God be interested in someone like her? Trying to put her friend off, Donna came up with an idea of her own.

"If you start a mums and tots group at the mission, then I'll go."

"Promise?"

"Promise," Donna replied, believing that it would never happen. She felt safe. Now her friend would leave off asking her to go to church. A month or two passed, and no more was said, until one day Donna was shocked by the unexpected.

"We're starting our mums and tots group on Tuesday, Donna; will you come?"

What could she say? She had promised. The baby smiled as Donna pushed the buggy towards the Dublin Christian Mission hall for the first time. She had plucked up the courage to go, and although the palpitations were almost choking her and the perspiration dripping from her forehead, Donna pushed open the door of the former community health clinic that was now the base of the work of the mission. It wasn't fancy; in fact, it was quite the opposite, but Donna felt welcome the minute she stepped inside.

The morning flew by as the mothers talked together about their babies, and teething, and nappy rash and the cost of living. They laughed, enjoying one another's company as much as the tea and biscuits. As the conversation died down, one of the mission workers started to talk about God. Of course, Donna had heard it all before – sure, the nuns had beaten it into them at school.

"God is everywhere."

She knew that.

"Because of what Jesus did on the cross, God can live in your heart," the girl continued.

Donna sat bolt upright. She had never heard *that* before! The talk continued, but Donna was in a world of her own, her mind silently carrying on a conversation with the speaker and God.

God live in my *heart – no way! He wouldn't want to live inside me – not with all the stuff that's in there – all that dirty stuff! He couldn't, could he?* By now Donna was hanging on every word. The thought that God could live in her heart was a concept she had never heard before, but it excited her and gave her something she hadn't had for a long time – hope. So, as the talk was coming to an end, the woman asked that anyone who wanted God to live in their heart should put their hand up. Donna's hand shot up like a bullet from a gun.

Yes! Yes! Donna wanted God to live in her heart more than anything she had ever wanted in her life – but would he come? Her head was spinning and her heart thumping, as she bowed her head and asked God to forgive her sin and to come and live in her heart. In that instant Donna felt a warmth in her chest and a feeling of lightness going through her, clearing away all the darkness in her life. She knew she had been cleaned up on the inside, and now she felt God telling her that her painful past wasn't her fault.

The lies of a lifetime were being dissolved, one by one. It

wasn't her fault that the old man had interfered with her when she was three. It wasn't her fault that her ma didn't love her. It wasn't her fault that her da beat her. It wasn't her fault that her "adopted" brother had abused her for all those years. It wasn't her fault that he had abused her little sister when she wasn't at home. It wasn't her fault that she had been raped, beaten and abused all her life.

It wasn't her fault! And the accumulated guilt of the years floated away. In place of that guilt and her own personal sin, Donna experienced God's love flowing through her. It was overwhelming, overpowering and beautiful beyond description! She was loved and she knew it. Imagine: the first person to tell her that he really loved her was God!

When she later asked God to take away her addiction to cigarettes, he filled her with a sensation she described as something like Aero bubbles – light, airy and comforting – only better! That good feeling has remained to this day. Donna recognizes that it is the Holy Spirit's presence that has carried her through every moment, including the tragic deaths of her mother, brother and sister.

In a supernatural way, Donna knew that whatever happened in her life from that moment in the Dublin Christian Mission, she would never be the same again. She had met with the God of heaven and he now lived in her heart. And no one would ever be able to take that love from her.

Sitting in a small, brightly coloured kitchen, I looked into Donna's eyes. I was transfixed as she told me about the day God came into her life.

"All that happened to me before doesn't matter," she said. "I know that God loves me and that's all that matters. Now I know what love really is, and every day I live I know that God loves me! That's all I need."

And the glint in her eyes and the smile in her face told me that her words were true. Now the new, changed Donna is happy in her life, her home and with her family.

As we finished our chat, Donna leaned over the kitchen table and in her broad, thick Dublin accent, she said: "One day I'm going to meet him – up there," and she nodded towards the sky. "And when I do, he's going to shake me by the hand and say: 'I know you – you'll do – come on in!'"

"No man has ever treated me like that!"

But then there has never been another man like Jesus…

About "Loveless"

c. 2085 BC

Read for yourself the story of Hagar, as it is told in Genesis 16:1–16.

Other related Bible references:

Genesis 12:10–20 Abram and Sarai in Egypt

Genesis 18:1–15 Promise of a son to Abraham and Sarah (this was the second time that God promised he would give descendants to Abraham – see Genesis 12:2).

AD 1970–2002

Each of the stories in this book have personally brought me both tears and laughter, but listening to Donna tell her story evoked emotions of a deeper kind. Yet the horror, anger and sorrow I felt were all pushed aside, as Donna described her encounter with Jesus. The light in her eyes and the obvious joy in her life made me feel that I was in a special place, with a special woman. Thank you, Donna, and please don't ever forget that God knows your name!

I was introduced to Donna through staff of the Dublin Christian Mission. The Mission does an amazing work with the children and families of inner-city Dublin, many of whom have problems relating to poverty, homelessness, alcohol and drug abuse, combined with dysfunctional life situations. The DCM workers are a selfless and dedicated team. Thank you!

A note from the author

It never ceases to amaze me how totally relevant the Bible is to our lives today, even though its writings date back millennia. It is undeniably God's chosen form of communication to us, his creation.

And yet the Bible does not merely record how God has dealt and does deal with mankind, but also how he relates to individuals. God is a personal God. He is concerned about us on a one-to-one basis; and God has no favourites. From paupers to royalty, he treats us all the same. Hopefully, you will have seen that from the lives of the individuals that I have introduced you to in this book. Whether from centuries ago or living today, these individuals have demonstrated that God cares for us deeply – deeply enough to intervene on our behalf.

I know that from personal experience. As a young mother, in a very dark place, I was drawn to words from the prophet Isaiah in response to a plea for God's help. My husband and I had just been told that our firstborn baby, a little girl, had an incurable genetic condition that would render her disabled and result in a life that would "never be normal".

I was bereft; unsure of what lay ahead; unconvinced that this could ever be part of God's plan for my life – until God told me otherwise. Using the words of Isaiah 43:1, he said: "Fear not, for I have redeemed you; I have called you by your name

Catherine; you are mine." (NKJV, italics mine)

The thought that God knew my name was not new to me, but the reality of that fact deeply impacted my life at that moment. The Creator of the universe knew all about this little speck of dust called Catherine Campbell and cared enough to reveal himself to me when my life was falling apart.

Since that time, I have discovered that he is a God who desires to know personally those who feel they are nameless nobodies; to love those who feel unloved; to accept those who feel rejected; to give value to those who feel worthless; and ultimately to give hope through Christ to those who otherwise have none.

Reading through the Bible, I was introduced to many individuals whose lives were blighted by the most extreme circumstances. It is my observation that the centuries have made little difference to human heartache. Since the fall of man pain has been part of the human package, whilst running parallel is the unchanging love and grace of God for the broken.

Writing *God Knows Your Name* has been a huge learning curve for me and also an enormous pleasure, as I have studied in depth the lives of people from both the Old and New Testaments. Sometimes there was a substantial amount of text to work with, while at other times a story is told in a mere few verses. However, around those few verses lay the much more complicated lives of individuals who had homes, families, jobs and responsibilities. Researching how these lives might have been lived was undertaken very carefully, from a variety of dependable sources. Setting the stories in the correct sociological, political and religious context was not only fascinating but hugely enlightening, making the factual portion of the biblical account come alive.

I am grateful to many scholars for their books on biblical manners and customs, whilst atlases, encyclopaedias and commentaries also had extremely helpful insight to offer.

Along the way, I have taken great care to seek to stay true to the Bible text and have included the textual references for you to examine for yourself. I hope you enjoy reading the Bible even more than this book.

As I have mentioned at the close of each chapter, it has also been an enormous privilege to interview people who were willing to share their stories with me. Handling the issues of a person's heart was nerve-wracking, to say the least! It was my deep desire to treat each story with respect, and therefore accuracy was paramount. Saying "thank you" to these individuals seems so inadequate, but I say it anyway – thank you! I pray that these stories will bless others as they have blessed me (and more!).

I still feel so much of a novice as a writer, so it is no surprise that I acknowledge the fact that I couldn't have done it without the help of others.

A big thank you goes to all my family for their encouragement and prayers as I set out on this, my biggest venture to date. Also to friends who, having read *Under the Rainbow* and *Rainbows for Rainy Days*, challenged me so often with, "When's the next one coming out?" So here it is, and I hope you don't regret your words!

This manuscript wouldn't have been so easy to read without the unbelievable help of my husband Philip and my dear friend Liz Young, who were patient and kind with their proofreading!

Also Monarch's publisher, Tony Collins, has been so helpful in steering me along the right path. Thank you.

And to God my heavenly Father, I say: "Thank you for knowing my name! May individuals, in turn, come to rely on *your* name – the one that is above all others!"

Influential Women Wendy Virgo

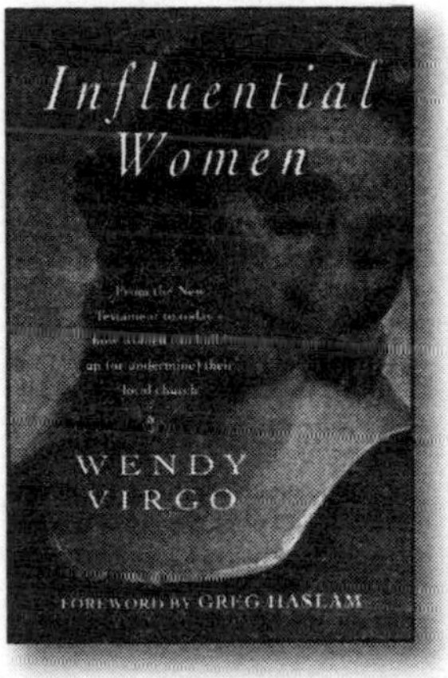

"Women are powerful in a church," writes Wendy Virgo. "They can be a tremendous asset – or a huge liability. They can influence the whole ambience of a church."

Here are Priscilla, Tabitha, Lois and Eunice, Euodia and Syntyche, and others. Some were saints, full of good works; some were frankly poisonous and did considerable harm. What can we learn?

"Wendy Virgo has an amazing gift for cheering on women in their faith in Jesus – and she does so with transparency, truth and tenderness. This is an encouraging and challenging read – buy it!"

– **Beth Redman,** writer and teacher, and leader of Soul Sista

"Wendy Virgo is a truly liberated woman who influences many churches today. Her cheerful nature, wisdom, and humility shine through this book."

– **Adrian Warnock**, blogger, adrianwarnock.com

"Wendy Virgo gives inspiring examples from the Bible and from her own lifetime of experience of how women can build up, rather than break down, the peace, unity and outreach of their church family."

– **Sharon James,** author, *God's Design for Women*

ISBN: 978-1-85424-921-0
Available from your local Christian bookshop.
In case of difficulty, please visit our website:
www.lionhudson.com